THE USBORNE INTRODUCTION
TO THE
FIRST
WORLD WAR

THE USBORNE INTRODUCTION
TO THE
FIRST WORLD WAR

Ruth Brocklehurst
& Henry Brook

Designed by Karen Tomlins
Michael Hill and Kate Rimmer

Edited by Jane Chisholm

Consultant: Terry Charman, Historian
Imperial War Museum

CONTENTS

A German plane flies over the pyramids, near Cairo. In 1915, German aircraft bombed Egypt, which was under British control at the time.

INTERNET LINKS

Look for the Internet Link boxes on the pages
of this book. They give descriptions of
interesting websites you can visit to find out
more about the First World War. For links to
these websites, go to the **Usborne Quicklinks
Website** at www.usborne-quicklinks.com
and type in the keywords "world war one"
You can find out more about how to use
Usborne Quicklinks at the back of this book.

THE WORLD AT WAR

The First World War was a human tragedy on a global scale. It began in Europe, but countries from around the world were soon dragged into the fighting. The war lasted for four dark years – from 1914 to 1918 – and a staggering 65 million men were mobilized to fight. Over 21 million people died, including 13 million civilians. The terrible impact of the war sparked revolutions, toppled once-great empires and changed the political map of Europe forever.

One of the poppy fields in northern France, where some of the bloodiest battles of the war took place. Many soldiers were struck by the beauty of the poppies that grew wild on the battlefields, and the poppy became a symbol for remembrance of the people who had died in the war.

THE GREAT WAR

The First World War was fought on such a massive scale that people called it the Great War. Never before had any war been fought on so many battlefields, with such a vast array of powerful and destructive weapons, and resulted in so many deaths.

Mass destruction

The reason the war was so destructive was that it was the first major war between the newly industrialized nations of Europe. In the days before factories, trains and steamships, wars often involved hundreds of men, charging into battle on foot or on horseback, brandishing swords. This time, it was possible to transport millions of men quickly to the front, and to arm them with an almost endless supply of the latest mass-produced weapons and ammunition. Machine guns, poison gas and barbed wire, as well as planes, tanks and submarines, all came into use – some for the first time – with devastating effect.

This map shows how, by August 1917, most of the world had divided into two sides in the war. On one side were the Allied Powers – shaded green on this map – and on the other were the Central Powers – shaded red. Only those places shaded yellow remained neutral.

Clash of empires

The most powerful countries involved had empires, with colonies and influence in every corner of the globe. So, although the war began in Europe, it rapidly spread to the wider world. Soon, men from the colonies were drawn into the fray. Beyond Europe, fighting took place on land – in Africa and Asia – and at sea – in the South Atlantic and the Pacific. Altogether, 28 countries became involved, making it the first war to be called a World War.

A German soldier is thrown from his feet by a powerful blast from a shell. This picture is from a movie made after the war, but with actors who fought in it.

Total war

The war affected the lives of civilians more than any previous war, because for the first time they were expected to help their country in the war effort. Workers had to step up agricultural and industrial production to keep their troops armed, clothed and fed.

All this meant that people far from the fighting became targets for enemy attack. Factories and supply routes were most at risk, but bombs fell on homes, schools and places of worship too. This kind of unrestricted warfare, in which whole populations are involved in the effort, is sometimes called Total War.

This map shows the European alliances during the First World War. The same shading is used throughout this book, to show which side each country was on.

INTERNET LINK

For a link to a website where you can explore an interactive timeline of the First World War, go to www.usborne-quicklinks.com

- Allied Powers
- Central Powers
- Neutral

SWEDEN

NORWAY

Christiania

Stockholm

Petrograd
(St. Petersburg)

North Sea

DENMARK

Copenhagen

Baltic Sea

UNITED KINGDOM

London

Amsterdam

The Hague   NETHERLANDS

Berlin

English Channel

Brussels

BELGIUM

GERMANY

RUSSIA

LUXEMBOURG

Paris

Luxembourg

Vienna

FRANCE

Bern

Budapest

SWITZERLAND

AUSTRIA-HUNGARY

Bay of Biscay

MONACO

RUMANIA
(Entered the war August 1916)

PORTUGAL
(Entered the war March 1916)

ANDORRA

ITALY
(Entered the war May 1915)

Adriatic Sea

BOSNIA

Belgrade

Bucharest

Black Sea

Sarajevo

SERBIA

BULGARIA
(Entered the war October 1915)

Madrid

Corsica
(Fr.)

MONTENEGRO

Rome

Cetinje

Sofia

Lisbon

SPAIN

Durazzo

Constantinople
(Istanbul)

Sardinia
(Ital.)

ALBANIA

GREECE
(Entered the war November 1916)

Aegean Sea

TURKISH EMPIRE
(Entered the war November 1914)

Mediterranean Sea

Sicily

Athens

Malta
(Br.)

Dodecanese Islands
(Ital.)

Crete

BALANCE OF POWER

Kaiser Wilhelm II was fascinated by the army, and loved dressing in uniform.

During the decades before 1914, Europe's most powerful nations split into two rival groups. The threat of war hung heavy in the air. Most governments hoped that the sheer size and strength of the two sides would prevent either one from attacking the other. But some began to fear that if Germany became stronger it might just tip this precarious balance of power. Then, a major war would be inevitable.

A nation is born

Until the late 19th century, Germany was made up of 39 small, independent states. In the 1870s, Prussia, the most powerful of them, led the German states in a successful invasion of northeast France, taking Alsace and Lorraine. Then, the Prussians convinced the other German states to unite with them, creating a powerful new nation.

The Central Powers

Fearing retaliation from France, the Germans formed an alliance with Austria-Hungary. They promised each other military aid if Russia attacked either of them, or helped another country, such as France, in a war against them. In 1882, Italy joined them to form a triple alliance known as the Central Powers. But, secretly, the Italians also made a pact with the French, to stay neutral if Germany invaded France.

Industrial superpower

The Germans wasted no time in building up their industries and expanding production of coal, iron and steel in their new nation. They were so ambitious that by 1913 they had outstripped Britain as Europe's leading industrial power.

The new ruler, Kaiser Wilhelm II, also had ambitions for a "place in the sun" to rival the empires of Britain and France. To do this, he expanded his army and ordered the construction of a new fleet of warships. By 1914, Germany had colonies in Africa, the Far East and the Pacific, and the second largest fleet in the world – after the British Royal Navy.

This 1914 German map of Europe shows Germany (blue) and Austria-Hungary (yellow) as determined soldiers, with weapons at the ready.

HMS *Dreadnought*, the battleship that started a costly arms race between Britain and Germany.

Three friends

During the 1890s, France and Russia became more and more worried about Germany's growing power, especially as the Kaiser had given important positions in his government to military officials. In 1893 they formed an alliance against Germany and the other Central Powers.

The British, too, began to fear that German expansion would threaten their empire and navy. So, in 1904, Britain and France signed the *Entente Cordiale* (meaning "Friendly Understanding") offering mutual aid in case of war. Three years later, Russia signed a similar agreement with Britain. The Triple Entente, as it was known, wasn't yet a strict military alliance, but later, they fought together as the Allied Powers, or Allies.

Arms race

As the two power blocks squared up to each other, the atmosphere between them became more and more tense. Governments across Europe began modernizing their armed forces and making plans for what to do if war did break out. The rivalry was at its fiercest in the naval arms race that grew up between Germany and Britain. In 1906, the British launched a new type of warship, named after the first of its kind – HMS *Dreadnought*. Powered by steam turbines and mounted with ten big guns, each with a range of 10km (6 miles) it was bigger, faster and had more firepower than any other battleship ever. The Germans soon began to build dreadnought-style ships of their own. By 1914, Britain had 30 dreadnoughts and Germany had built 20. War was looming on the horizon.

ASSASSINATION AND CRISIS

On Sunday June 28, 1914, disaster struck in the Bosnian capital of Sarajevo. A nineteen-year-old student shot Archduke Franz Ferdinand, the heir to the Austro-Hungarian throne. The assassination provided the spark that ignited the First World War.

Balkan belligerents

The Balkan states of southeastern Europe had a long history of wars and ethnic tension, going right back to the time of the Roman empire. During the 18th and 19th centuries, they had been fought over by two powerful empires: the Ottoman Turks and the Austro-Hungarians. Bosnia and Serbia had been ruled by the Turks until 1878, when Bosnia was handed over to Austria-Hungary and Serbia was granted independence. Since then, Serbia had expanded its territory and was beginning to pose a threat to Austrian power in the region.

This map shows the Balkan states in 1914, sandwiched between the two great empires of Austria-Hungary and Ottoman Turkey.

Most Bosnians and Serbs were Slavic people. Many of them wanted to bring an end to Austro-Hungarian rule in Bosnia so that they could unite their two countries and form an independent Slavic nation. Passions ran high, and some revolutionaries were prepared to go to extreme lengths to achieve this goal.

Franz Ferdinand and his wife Sophie in Sarajevo, about to climb into their car. Minutes later they would be shot dead.

Suicidal assassins

When the heir to the Austro-Hungarian throne, Archduke Franz Ferdinand, announced an official visit to Sarajevo, a Serbian terrorist organization called the Black Hand decided it was time to strike. It recruited and trained three Bosnian student activists, and armed them with pistols, hand bombs and cyanide capsules. Their mission was to assassinate the Archduke, then to commit suicide so that the killing could not be linked to the Black Hand. The young Bosnians – Gavrilo Princip, Nedjelko Cabrinovic and Trifco Grabez – were all dying slowly of tuberculosis. Their lives seemed a small price to pay for what they believed to be a just cause.

Gavrilo Princip: the Bosnian teenager who unwittingly started the First World War. He received a twenty year sentence, but died in prison, of tuberculosis, on April 28, 1918.

Police seize one of the Bosnian assasins on June 28, 1914. For many years this picture was said to show the arrest of Gavrilo Princip, but it is now thought to be Nedjelko Cabrinovic.

Royal murder

When Franz Ferdinand and his wife Sophie arrived in Sarajevo, they were driven to a reception with the Governor of Bosnia. The streets were lined with well-wishers cheering the Archduke as he waved from an open-top car. But hidden among the crowds were the three assassins, and four accomplices, intent on murder. As the motorcade passed Nedjelko Cabrinovic, he hurled his bomb. It missed Franz Ferdinand's car, but hit the one behind, injuring its passengers and several onlookers. Chaos spread through the crowd, as the imperial party sped for the safety of the City Hall. For now, the plot had failed.

After the reception, the Archduke decided to visit those injured in the earlier attack. His driver took a wrong turn, right past Gavrilo Princip, who seized his chance. Grabbing his pistol, he fired at almost point-blank range, shooting Franz Ferdinand in the neck and Sophie in the abdomen. The driver raced back to the Governor's residence, but the Archduke and his wife died before they could receive medical help.

INTERNET LINK

For a link to a website where you can watch film footage of Franz Ferdinand in Sarajevo on the day he was assassinated, go to www.usborne-quicklinks.com

Taking the blame

Princip and Cabrinovic both swallowed their cyanide, but the poison failed and they were arrested, along with their accomplices. Under interrogation, they soon revealed that the Black Hand had orchestrated the assassination.

The Austrians insisted that the Serbian government should take responsibility for the Black Hand's actions. They issued them with a strict set of demands. When the Serbs failed to meet all these demands, Austria-Hungary, with German backing, declared war on Serbia on July 28. Tensions between the European powers now came to a head. The die was cast.

13

EUROPE IN ARMS

As news of the assassination spread across Europe, few people could have imagined the impact it would have. But when the Germans offered their unconditional support to Austria-Hungary, the complex web of European alliances came into play. What had started as a local crisis triggered a chain of events that sent Europe careering headlong into full-scale war.

Two British soldiers – nick-named 'Tommies' – board a train at London's Victoria Station, bound for France.

German forces moved swiftly to seize the Belgian capital, Brussels, in the first month of the war.

Domino effect

Within days of Austria's declaration of war on Serbia, Europe's military leaders put their war plans into action. On July 31, the Russians announced that they were moving their army into position, ready to help their Serbian allies against Austria-Hungary, if necessary. The Germans saw this as an act of aggression. So, on August 1, they declared war on Russia. The French, in turn, rallied their troops to support the Russians. This provoked the Germans to declare war on France on August 3.

The Schlieffen Plan

Germany was now at war with France to the west and Russia to the east. War on two fronts would mean splitting the army in two, weakening its effectiveness. But, back in 1899, the military commander Alfred von Schlieffen had anticipated this problem and had prepared a plan. His theory was that Russian troops would take at least six weeks to get ready to cross the German frontier, because their vast country had a very poor rail network. This would give the Germans plenty of time to defeat France, on the Western Front, before dealing with Russia, on the Eastern Front. On August 4, 1914, the German army put the Schlieffen Plan into action. They marched into Belgium, heading for Paris by the shortest, flattest route.

Britain enters the war

The Germans did not expect Britain, the world's greatest sea power, to join a European land war. But, by invading Belgium, they made a big mistake. Belgium was a neutral country, and Britain had a long-standing treaty to protect it. The German chancellor considered the agreement a mere "scrap of paper" – but the British took it more seriously. Belgium's ports provided a vital link between Britain and the rest of Europe. If the Germans captured them, it would severely harm British trade and security in the English Channel. Eleven hours after the invasion, Britain declared war on Germany.

A family affair

Europe was up in arms, but many people still believed that diplomatic talks could defuse the situation. The British king, George V, Tsar Nicholas II of Russia and Kaiser Wilhelm II, were all grandsons of Queen Victoria, and early August saw a flurry of telegrams sent from one cousin to another. They were convinced that their close relationship would make a war between their countries impossible. But it was too late to stop the military advance that had been set in motion.

Queen Victoria – the 'Grandmama of Europe' – sits at the heart of her extended family. Seated on the left is Kaiser Wilhelm II, behind him in a bowler hat is Tsar Nicholas II. Behind the Tsar is his uncle, the future Edward VII, father of George V.

PLANS UNRAVEL

As the fighting began, army commanders put into action war plans made years before. But neither the plans, nor the men's training, took into account the massive advances made in weapons technology during the previous two decades. By the end of the first month's fighting, it was clear that the war was not going to go according to plan. New weapons would mean a new kind of war.

This huge 'Big Bertha' siege gun could fire an 820kg (1,800 pounds) shell over 15km (9 miles).

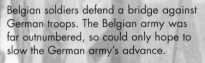

Belgian soldiers defend a bridge against German troops. The Belgian army was far outnumbered, so could only hope to slow the German army's advance.

Big guns in Belgium

For the Schlieffen Plan to work, the German army chief of staff, Helmuth von Moltke, needed his troops to push through Belgium and on to Paris as quickly as possible. But the Belgians put up an unexpectedly stubborn resistance from their forts around the city of Liège. They inflicted heavy losses on the Germans and slowed their progress. But, eventually, Moltke's troops smashed through the forts, using their secret weapon – a massive siege cannon known as Big Bertha. After that, they swept through Belgium, terrorizing soldiers and civilians alike.

> ### INTERNET LINK
>
> For a link to a website where you can view an animated map of the German advance to Paris and the opening battles of the war, go to **www.usborne-quicklinks.com**

German troops enter French territory, pushing through woodland in the Argonne region.

Battling on the frontiers

As the Germans advanced through Belgium, a British force of about 100,000 men landed in France and clashed with the Germans near the Belgian town of Mons. At the same time, the French launched Plan XVII – their strategy to take back Alsace and Lorraine – with a series of offensives along the Franco-German frontier, that became known as the Battle of the Frontiers.

At this stage, the pace of the war was rapid and exhausting. Armies were constantly on the move across vast battlefields. It was the first time many of the soldiers had faced machine guns and chaotic battles were fought under a hail of bullets. The Allies were outnumbered and outgunned at every turn. The French, fighting in red and blue uniforms, made easy targets and suffered huge casualties. Forced to retreat, they abandoned their Plan XVII. Now they were fighting to save Paris itself.

Russian sacrifice

To the east, Russian forces moved quicker than the Germans had expected. On August 4, they invaded East Prussia (now northern Poland), where there was only a small German army. This forced Moltke to divert 100,000 troops away from France. On August 26, the Germans began their counterattack, driving the Russians into dense woodland near Tannenberg. There, in just four days, Russia suffered one of the most crushing defeats of the war, with around 60,000 casualties. The Germans captured some 92,000 Russian soldiers and 500 guns. After further defeats at the Masurian Lakes, the Russian army retreated from East Prussia for good.

Fighting for Paris

Despite the Russian diversion, the Germans had come within 40km (25 miles) of Paris. The French government fled, along with a million Parisians, leaving the rest to prepare for a siege. On September 3, the French commander-in-chief of the Allied troops, Joseph Joffre, ordered his men to take up a defensive position along the River Marne. Three days later, the Battle of the Marne began.

Strengthened by extra British troops and French reinforcements, transported from Paris in a fleet of taxis, the Allies now had the advantage. Their exhausted German opponents had marched more than 240km (150 miles) and were running out of supplies. By September 9, the battle had turned against them and they began to retreat. The Schlieffen Plan had failed, and Paris was saved.

Under French escort, some of the 29,000 German troops captured during the fighting on the Marne are marched into captivity.

OVER BY CHRISTMAS?

During the opening months of the war, thousands of men throughout Europe enthusiastically volunteered to fight, confident that it would be a quick, clean contest, and that they would all be home for Christmas. But, by October 1914, armies on both sides stopped advancing as they were ordered to dig trenches all along the Western Front, the German frontier with Belgium and France. The fighting rapidly reached stalemate. As winter set in, soldiers realized they faced a long and bloody fight in the mud.

Excited French troops wave from a train as they leave Paris for the front, August 1914.

CARVING A NEW FRONTIER

With the German army in retreat after the Battle of the Marne, the ambitious Schlieffen Plan was in tatters. Desperate to turn the situation back to their advantage, Kaiser Wilhelm appointed General Erich von Falkenhayn as overall commander, in place of General von Moltke. But Moltke had one final order for his exhausted troops: to "fortify and defend" their positions above the River Aisne. This simple instruction would change the whole course of the war.

The ground where the Allies dug their first trenches was very wet and prone to flooding.

The line hardens

The German armies halted their retreat at the Chemin des Dames Ridge. They turned this 40km (25 miles) long wedge of high ground into a fortress, protected by a network of trenches, barbed wire and machine gun posts. When the British and French attacked the ridge on September 14, they were stopped dead in their tracks. Caught without shelter from the German guns, the Allies started digging their own defensive trenches. Amazingly, they would still be living in these crumbling earthworks four years later, fighting over much the same shell-scarred battlefield.

On the offensive

Frustrated by the hold-up at the Chemin des Dames Ridge, the Allies changed their tactics. The country to the north of it lay open. If the French could rush an army around the side, or flank, of Falkenhayn's troops, they would be able to cut the German supply lines and capture the ridge. But Falkenhayn had his own plans for the gap in the north. He ordered his generals to outflank the British and seize the Channel ports of Calais, Dunkirk and Boulogne, only 160km (100 miles) away. His soldiers could then march on Paris and snatch a stunning victory for their new commander.

As the Germans retreated to the Aisne, they blew up bridges behind them, making it difficult for the British and French to pursue them.

Plugging the gaps

Both sides scrambled north, in what became known as the Race to the Sea. They fought battles and dug trenches along the way, marking their progress across the Belgian region of Flanders. But the race ended in a frustrating draw, as the opposing armies arrived at the dark waters of the North Sea, before either could win an advantage. Falkenhayn's generals found what they thought was a weak point in the British-held territory, at the Belgian town of Ypres. There, in late October, they launched a desperate attack.

A taste of things to come

The Battle of Ypres was a bloody and disastrous introduction to trench fighting for all concerned. The British were outnumbered, outgunned, and ill-prepared, but they still managed to hold their ground. The German infantry suffered terrible casualties, losing whole battalions of young recruits as they charged across open fields to their deaths.

The fighting finally sputtered out at the end of November, when heavy rains turned the battlefield to mud, and ammunition supplies ran low. Still in Allied hands, Ypres would be the setting for years of bitter fighting and another two major battles. Already, at least 50,000 German and 24,000 British troops lay dead in Flanders fields.

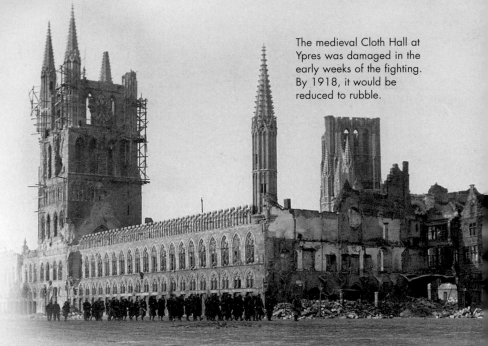

The medieval Cloth Hall at Ypres was damaged in the early weeks of the fighting. By 1918, it would be reduced to rubble.

Trench-lock

The fast-paced fighting of the previous months now ground to a standstill. Trenches stretched out from the Chemin des Dames ridge in a jagged scar, across northern Europe. This border between armies was known as the Western Front. It snaked 765km (475 miles) from the Belgian coast to the mountains of Switzerland. Millions of men guarded their dirt fortifications, with the industrial might of Europe's nations gearing up behind them. The long years of deadlock in the trenches had only just begun.

BATTLES
1. Mons (Aug. 1914)
2. Marne (Sept. 1914)
3. First Ypres (Oct. 1914)
4. Arras (Oct. 1914)
5. Neuve Chapelle (March 1915)
6. Second Ypres (May 1915)
7. Loos (Sept. 1915)

This map shows the main battlefields of the Western Front during the first year of fighting. By this time, most of the front line was scored with trenches.

FIRE, WIRE AND MUD

Commanders on both sides believed the war in the trenches would be short-lived. But, they were used to fighting in the open, with armies charging at each other across huge battlefields. The shelter of the trenches, combined with the destructive power of modern weapons, made it impossible for either side to break through in the old way. In the winter of 1914, whole armies ground to a halt. They would spend years locking horns in the mud.

Killing evolves

The tactics and weapons used in an attack hadn't changed much since the 19th century, but defending troops had a range of new and deadly tools at their disposal. Their rifles, machine guns and high explosive shells ripped any attacking infantry to shreds. This firepower could have destroyed the warring armies in less than a year, if it hadn't been for the shelter offered by the trenches.

This is a detail from **Over the top** by John Nash, an official war artist for the British government. The stark scene depicts the artist's own experience of war in the trenches.

INTERNET LINK

For a link to a website where you can play a game to defend a trench and choose the equipment you might need on different missions, go to **www.usborne-quicklinks.com**

Steel brambles

The trenches may have been filthy, uncomfortable and dangerous places, but they did offer some protection from enemy fire. German military engineers took particular care designing their trenches. Their front line was a labyrinth of ditches, tunnels and deep shelters that protected soldiers from explosive shells. They were also quick to lay thick beds of razor-sharp barbed wire to protect their trenches. It was hard to cut by hand and exploding shells only lifted it off the ground and dropped it down in a tangled and impenetrable mess. So, for both sides, it was easy to defend a position, but almost impossible to attack it successfully.

Going over the top

But, even after the slaughter at Ypres, many generals were still convinced that by shelling enemy positions, then sending waves of attacking infantry, they would eventually break the enemy line and force a return to fighting in the open. However, millions of men would die testing this theory in the blood-soaked years to come. The order to go 'over the top' meant that soldiers had to scramble out of their trenches and charge straight into enemy fire.

Into the void

On the night before an infantry attack, thousands of soldiers gathered at the front. They could hear their own shells screaming overhead and crashing into enemy lines. If all went according to plan, the barrage would clear a path through the barbed wire and kill most of the defenders, but it rarely did. The open ground between the trench lines, known as no-man's-land, was a strip of broken, desolate earth, stripped bare of any vegetation by shellfire. It could be anything from shouting distance across, to 5km (3 miles) wide.

In most attacks, commanders lost sight of their men the moment they climbed up into the smoke and confusion of no-man's-land. The only way to give them new orders was by messenger, or by means of an experimental telephone system that used buried wires. But messengers were shot down as they sprinted back and forth, and high-explosive shells slamming into the ground cut the telephone wires. It could take hours for an officer to receive vital orders, while the situation around him was changing by the second.

In the first years of the war, soldiers were ordered not to run or zigzag as they crossed no-man's-land. Generals thought troops might get confused and panic if they didn't advance in orderly ranks. But this only made it easier for enemy machine gunners to mow them down in neat lines.

In this painting, French troops make the terrifying journey across no-man's-land, past tangles of barbed wire to attack enemy trenches.

GOING UP THE LINE

The Germans were the first to dig in, seizing any available high, dry ground. All along the Western Front, they held the best positions. The Allied soldiers had to dig wherever their advance ended, even where the earth was boggy or rock-hard. Their trenches were often shallow and easily flooded. But, wet or dry, every man sheltering in the dirt shared the same daily terrors.

INTERNET LINK

For a link to a website where you can explore a panoramic reconstruction of a trench system, go to
www.usborne-quicklinks.com

First impressions

Just getting to the trenches was an ordeal in itself. New soldiers usually arrived by train at a rest area, located miles behind the front line. Then, they marched to the front at night, when there was less risk of being spotted by enemy gunners. Approaching the battle zone, they passed along shattered roads, through ruined villages and forests of splintered trees, until their path dipped and narrowed and they entered a communication trench. These long, twisting ditches were the arteries for all the supplies and fresh troops that fed into the trench network.

The combat zone

After months of shelling, some communication trenches were so torn and featureless that arriving soldiers needed guides to lead them. It was easy to get lost when all you could see was the night sky and bare mud walls. Frightened and disorientated, the men reached the reserve trenches first. There were usually one or two of these running in parallel to the front line and they were used as work areas and fallback positions in case of an attack. But the soldiers' final destination was the fire trench, bordering no-man's-land. Here they were greeted by an overwhelming stench of unburied corpses, gun smoke and open latrines – the pits that served as toilets.

Mud and rain meant the trenches needed constant maintenance. These British men taking a rest from digging are wrapped up in a variety of hats, scarves and furs, sent from home to keep them warm.

Mind your head

Soldiers quickly learned to keep their ears open and their heads down at all times. It was rare for a trench to be much deeper than head height. This only added to feelings of tension and claustrophobia, as thousands of soldiers died from head wounds. It was only late in 1915 that French troops were issued with steel helmets; the British didn't receive them until 1916. The army used the euphemistic term 'wastage' to describe the daily losses in the trenches.

Constant companions

There were other, ever-present hazards – rain and snow, plagues of vermin and disease. Thousands of soldiers died of exposure or lost their feet to a fungal infection known as trench foot. Body lice made the men itch and gave them fevers. Huge rats gorged themselves on the dead, and one German officer described flies so thick on the ground they looked like a cushion of blue velvet.

Soldiers had to manage with all this as best they could, as they lived in the fire trench for a week or two at a time. Then, they would spend another week in a support trench, before replacements came and they could go back to the reserve area for a week or two, before the cycle began again.

The lay of the land

People tend to think of trenches as being straight, but in fact they were made up of short, straight sections – called traverses – linked together at right angles. This meant that soldiers could dodge around a corner to shelter from bullets or shrapnel from shells, whatever angle they were coming from. Piles of sandbags formed a 'parapet' along the front of the trenches, to give cover from snipers. More sandbags at the back formed a 'parados' to protect the men from shells exploding behind them, and shots fired from the reserve trenches.

Reserve trench

Support trench

Fire trench

Communication trenches

Barbed wire

NO-MAN'S-LAND

Shell holes

Fire trench

This diagram shows the typical layout of the trenches. By the end of the war, there were over 32,200km (20,000 miles) of these snaky systems carved out of the Western Front.

A STORM OF STEEL

The single biggest killer in the First World War was artillery fire. It churned up the ground, ripped men apart and buried them alive under mounds of earth. In the days leading up to a big infantry attack, artillery teams bombarded enemy positions with millions of high-explosive shells. As far away as London, people could hear the roar of the guns in northern France – the distant thunder of an industrialized war.

Making shells in a munitions factory was a hazardous job, as accidental explosions were a constant danger.

On the assembly line

For hundreds of years, warring armies had used artillery to fire cannonballs and other missiles. But, in the decades leading up to the First World War, scientists began combining advances in weapons technology with the manufacturing power of huge factories. Thousands of guns rolled off the production lines. And they were bigger, easier to fire and deadlier than ever.

INTERNET LINK

For a link to a website where you can find out more about all the weapons used in the war, and see pictures of many of them, go to www.usborne-quicklinks.com

Canadian soldiers loading a howitzer artillery gun. Such weapons were designed to fire a shell high into the air so it plunged down on a trench or fort with deadly, penetrating force.

A hundred ways to die

These artillery weapons were only part of the new and terrifying arsenal of killing machines. In the trenches, there were a hundred different ways to die. Hand grenades had been around for years, but new varieties were developed during the war. These were safer for the soldier throwing them, but they caused terrible injuries in cramped trenches. Both sides also used flame-throwers to send jets of fire into enemy positions.

Machine guns were also in use by this time, and their fire cut through attacking infantry like a scythe. In 1885, an American inventor, Hiram Maxim, had harnessed the energy released by a shooting bullet to load the next round in an instant. Belts of bullets fed into the gun so it could fire 500 rounds every minute. Bullets could maim and kill, but what soldiers feared far more was shrapnel and high-explosive shells. They were used in an attempt to destroy enemy trenches in advance of an infantry attack.

German soldiers on the edge of an Allied trench. Standing up to throw a grenade, as the man on the left is doing, exposed a soldier to terrible risk from enemy fire.

New ways of killing

Artillery shells were packed with recently invented explosives, like dynamite or TNT, and came in a fearful range of shapes and sizes. Shrapnel shells burst into hundreds of razor-sharp fragments before they hit the ground, slicing through flesh and bone. The shrapnel often picked up dirt before entering the body, causing fatal infections and blood poisoning. The effects of high-explosives were even more terrifying – they could rip a man to tiny pieces. Massive siege shells were designed not to explode until they'd smashed through a fort's stone and steel fortifications.

Perfect timing

Even with all the improvements in artillery, army gunners still had a difficult task. They had to fire test shots to find the right target. This gave trench defenders plenty of warning before raids. There were problems with faulty shells that didn't explode, known as duds, while poor communications sometimes resulted in barrages falling too late or too early to be of much use to the attackers. It would take years for gunners to achieve the perfect timing and accuracy needed to protect infantry as they attacked – a key tactic that would eventually help to unlock the Western Front.

1915.
AUBERS RIDGE.
FESTUBERT.
LOOS.
1916.
THE BLUFF YPRES.

GHOSTS, SHADOWS AND LIES

Life in the trenches could be a strange and bewildering experience. The heat and haze of battle sometimes played tricks with a soldier's eyes, making it hard to make out what was real or imaginary. Fantastic stories and superstitions were whispered among the troops, the eerie myths of a disturbing war.

A last goodbye

In sections of trench where there was heavy fighting, soldiers lived alongside the unburied bodies of dead friends and enemy fighters. In this hellish landscape of corpses and mud, soldiers regularly reported seeing ghosts of missing pals returning to see their old posts and comrades. Back at home, some families reported surprise visits from male relatives, apparently at the very moment when they had been killed on the battlefield.

Phantom warriors

Other ghosts got stuck into the fighting. After the Battle of Mons in August 1914, British troops were buzzing with stories of a lost platoon guided to safety by a friendly phantom. The idea that the spirit world was on their side must have appealed to the men. They had been outnumbered and outgunned, and some of the soldiers believed that they had only been saved by a troop of warrior angels, who appeared to fire flaming arrows at the Germans.

The myth was probably based on a ghost story, published in a newspaper in 1914. In it, the British army was aided by Saint George and a host of angels. The author of the tale, Arthur Machen, denied suggestions that it was based on real events, but many people refused to accept that it was all make-believe. Similar myths of ghostly patriots remained popular throughout the war.

ANGEL OF MONS Valse

by PAUL PAREE.

This 1916 illustration of the Angel of Mons is from the cover of the sheet music for a waltz inspired by the legend.

The body factory

Myths had a powerful effect on soldiers' morale and on how they felt about the enemy. In 1917, British soldiers heard whispers about a secret, ghoulish factory where the Germans turned their war dead into explosives and fertilizer. The story was so powerful, that it helped to convince the Chinese to declare war on Germany in August 1917. It was only when the fighting was over that a British army officer admitted the story was a propaganda lie, to make the Germans sound like monsters.

> INTERNET LINK
>
> For a link to a website where you can read Arthur Machen's ghost story 'The Bowmen' in full, go to **www.usborne-quicklinks.com**

Albert's Angel

Soldiers marching off to war are always on the lookout for good or bad omens. Thousands of men passed through the town of Albert on their way to the front, gazing in amazement at the cathedral. A statue of the Virgin Mary holding the Christ Child topped the cathedral's tower. But because the tower offered commanding views of the battlefield, it was a prime target for enemy gunners. A shell had knocked the statue over, and for years it hung at a bizarre angle. Many soldiers believed that when the statue finally crashed to earth the fighting would end, and the side responsible would lose the war.

The statue of Mary hangs perilously from the cathedral tower in Albert. Eventually, she was toppled by British gunners in 1918, proving the myth to be false.

Cloud ships

High explosive shells could create amazing light effects and the gasses they produced may even have affected local weather. At Gallipoli, in August 1915, British survivors of one battle described how a whole battalion of 800 men had vanished inside a mysterious, glowing cloud that carried them away without a trace.

Several years passed before the myth was explained. A Turkish farmer was clearing some thick woodland a few miles from the battlefield when he discovered the bodies of hundreds of dead British soldiers, their bones strewn among the trees. The lost battalion had marched through the mist into wild country, where they had been ambushed by the enemy, and wiped out to the last man.

NORTH SEA RAIDERS

While opposing armies fought it out in the mud, British and German battleships prowled the waters of the North Sea. Most people expected a quick showdown between the two fleets in the grand tradition of previous wars. But the war at sea began with another tried and tested tactic: naval blockade.

A Royal Navy signalman on board a British warship. The position of his flags spell out different letters of the alphabet.

Stranglehold

The British navy set up a blockade around Europe the moment war was declared, searching merchant ships and confiscating cargos bound for Germany. German chemists invented substitutes for goods that would have been imported – explosives, fertilizers, even coffee. But food rationing still had to be introduced and people struggled to find enough to eat. German admirals were desperate to smash the blockade, but most of their fleet was trapped inside the North Sea by British warships. Only their submarines – known as *U-boats* – could slip past the patrols. So in February 1915 they ordered the U-boats to sink any ship sighted in British coastal waters.

Warring fleets

In the years leading up to the war, Britain and Germany had spared no expense improving and expanding their fleets. Their 'big gun' dreadnoughts were paraded at sea, symbols of naval might, supported by an armada of other warships. Battle cruisers were lighter and faster than dreadnoughts, but still packed a powerful punch. Smaller vessels, such as destroyers, patrolled coastal seas.

Flying the flag

Ships were fitted with wireless radio sets that could send long-distance sound signals. As they were easy to intercept, messages were usually sent in code. But, it could take up to ten minutes to decipher and rush a message to a captain. So in battle conditions the fleets still relied on traditional flag signals to communicate between ships. This system was fine in slow, close-quarter battles back in the days when warships were powered by sail. But modern navies could be strung out for miles across the ocean, almost hidden by smoke and spray. Communication foul-ups sometimes ended in disaster.

Battle of the Bight

The British fleet struck first, sending a small group of cruisers and destroyers to attack German patrols in the Heligoland Bight on August 28, 1914. They sank two torpedo boats and a destroyer, and then lured a pack of pursuing enemy cruisers into the North Sea. British warships steamed up to sink three of these cruisers, and over 700 German sailors lost their lives.

Ship to shore

On November 3, the German navy began to turn its guns on British coastal towns and Great Yarmouth was shelled. Then, on December 16, their warships attacked Scarborough, Hartlepool and Whitby. Whitby's clifftop abbey was left in ruins and 139 people were killed before the raiders slipped safely back to base. The raids outraged the country and embarrassed the Royal Navy, who saw itself as the nation's protector.

Message received

In January 1915, the British navy struck again. They had recovered three codebooks from wrecked and captured German ships and were able to use this incredible good luck to read intercepted radio signals. On the night of January 23, they decoded an enemy message describing a raid planned for the morning. When German warships crossed an area called Dogger Bank in the middle of the North Sea, the British were waiting for them – in force.

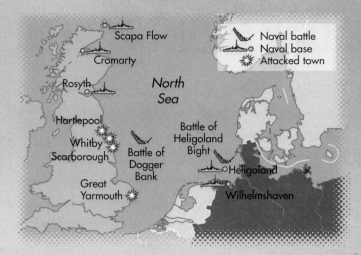

The North Sea, showing the major battle sites in the early stages of the war, British and German naval bases and the British towns that were subjected to naval bombardment.

Disaster at Dogger Bank

The Germans tried to run, but there was no escape from the long-range guns of the British ships. Four German warships were caught at Dogger Bank. One, the *Blücher*, was sunk, and another badly damaged. On the British side, HMS *Lion* had to be towed back to port, but only 15 sailors had been killed. The German fleet had lost over a thousand men. It was a clear win for the British, but the war at sea was only just beginning.

German sailors cling to the side of the warship *Blücher*, as it capsizes at Dogger Bank. Many of the men who ended up in the cold waters of the North Sea in January would have died from exposure.

YOUR COUNTRY NEEDS YOU

The European powers had spent the years leading up to the war expanding and modernizing their armed forces, but few were ready by the time the fighting broke out. As the death toll in the trenches mounted, thousands more soldiers were sent to the front. Some were battle-hardened professionals, but for many others this would be their first ever taste of armed conflict.

The design of this 1914 British recruitment poster of Lord Kitchener has been much imitated ever since.

The call-up

By 1914, many young men in Europe were required to serve a short period of military service, known as conscription. This meant that countries like Germany and France already had reserves of trained soldiers to call on when the war broke out. The German army was the most efficient in the world; it began the war with a force of 4,500,000 men, all fully equipped. In the first weeks of the war, the French called up reserve troops and fighters from their colonies in North Africa, raising a force of 4,017,000 men.

Some men recruited in London underwent their training in the streets because there was a shortage of army barracks.

Friends and brothers

At the outbreak of the war, Britain didn't have conscription, and its army was far smaller than that of France. Lord Kitchener, Secretary of State for War, needed to raise a new army, so he quickly appealed for volunteers. He knew men would be more likely to sign up if they could train and fight alongside their friends, so he set up so-called 'Pals Battalions' – groups of men from the same city, village or workplace. He also relied heavily on colonial troops. Within just two months, a spectacular 761,000 men had answered the call.

German reservists get ready to go to the front. Their children have borrowed their distinctive spiked helmets.

Suited and booted

Soldiers on both sides were equipped with much the same basic kit to take to the front, but their uniforms were more varied. In the late 19th century, the British army had replaced its traditional scarlet with a less conspicuous khaki brown. Germany and Russia soon opted for muted shades too. The French marched to war in red trousers, making them easy targets at the Battle of Marne. After that, they adopted a dull blue. Despite these changes, some troops held on to regional elements of dress.

These illustrations are from a German poster of Allied uniforms in 1914. Among them are a French Zouave (from Algeria) in baggy pants and a red fez, a British Highlander dressed in a kilt, a Sikh in his turban and a Russian Cossack wearing a tall astrakhan hat.

The gentle art of persuasion

Even where there was conscription, governments went to great lengths to encourage young men to volunteer. Propaganda posters, leaflets and newspaper articles were all designed to build patriotic feelings and public enthusiasm for the war. Some campaigns were targeted at women, suggesting that they should persuade, or shame, their menfolk into enlisting. Some men, known as conscientious objectors, refused to fight because it was against their moral or religious beliefs. But the pressure to sign up was immense – anyone not in uniform was branded a coward.

French   British   Russian

A DAY OF PEACE

The first winter in the trenches was brutally cold. Soldiers sat through snowstorms, frosts and flash floods. But, despite the fighting and the weather raging around them, some men were determined to celebrate Christmas Day – even if it meant stopping the war to do it.

Royal presents

People at home didn't want the troops to think they'd been forgotten. Princess Mary, the daughter of the British king, set up a Christmas fund for sailors and soldiers. People gave so generously that the fund was able to send everyone in British uniform a special gift. This became known as the Princess Mary Box. It was a brass box crammed with tobacco and chocolates.

The Kaiser sent his men pipes, cigars, and more festive presents: tiny Christmas trees. Decking a tree was an old tradition in Germany, but when British soldiers south of Ypres saw lights and strange shapes moving about in the opposite trench, they wondered if there was a night attack coming. It was only when they heard the carol singing across no-man's-land that they realized the Germans were just celebrating Christmas.

German soldiers on the Eastern Front sing carols around a Christmas tree. They are lucky to be well behind the front line. There was no truce on the Eastern Front. For most, Christmas was just like any other day of fighting in the trenches.

Meeting halfway

Slowly, and more out of curiosity than anything else, men began to peer out of the trenches. Soon, soldiers on both sides were stepping into no-man's-land. It didn't take long for the rival soldiers to strike up conversations. They suggested having a short cease-fire – a truce so they could come out and bury their dead. As the sun came up on Christmas Day, crowds of soldiers could be seen in the middle of the battlefield. Men came face-to-face with their enemies, most of them unarmed and eager to shake hands.

Two of Princess Mary's boxes of presents for the fighting men of Britain

A day in the open

The soldiers shared stories and traded tobacco or buttons from their uniforms. A man who had been a barber before the war offered haircuts to all comers for the price of a few cigarettes. In one section of the line, the two sides even played a friendly match of soccer.

But, as night fell, the men returned to their posts in the trenches. In most sections of the Western Front, the Christmas Truce lasted little more than a few hours. It was a pause in the battle, rather than a genuine peace. But it gave the soldiers an opportunity to get a glimpse of their enemy and to bury their dead comrades.

INTERNET LINK

For a link to a website where you can read eyewitness accounts of the Christmas Truce of 1914, go to
www.usborne-quicklinks.com

United in adversity, British and German soldiers meet in no-man's-land on Christmas day, 1914. For a few short hours they exchanged cigarettes, food, even hats, and talked together.

Live and let live

The generals on both sides were furious when they heard about the festive cease-fire. In the years that followed, army authorities made sure that such a truce would not happen again. The truce of 1914 involved thousands of men, mainly in the German and British trenches, but there were hundreds of smaller unofficial cease-fires at other times during the war. Soldiers would catapult messages between the trenches, agreeing not to fire their guns at certain times of the day or giving advance warning of artillery attacks. This was known as 'live and let live' and it usually only lasted a few days, until an officer realized what was happening and ordered his men to behave more aggressively.

GOING GLOBAL

Right from the start, the Great War was destined to become a global conflict. Britain, France and Germany all had colonies around the world, which soon became targets for enemy attack. The war grew wider still, as Japan and the Ottoman Turkish empire entered the fray. By the end of 1914, fighting had erupted in the Far East, the South Atlantic, Africa, Central Asia and the Middle East.

South African mounted troops, fighting for the British, prepare to advance into German South West Africa.

CRUISER WARFARE

While fighting on the Western Front became concentrated on a small area on either side of the trenches, the war at sea ranged far and wide. The German navy only had a small fleet of cruisers outside the North Sea, but its commanders were talented and determined. They hoped an aggressive campaign against the Allies' ports, merchant ships and military vessels would weaken their economies and Britain's dominance of global waters.

Oriental offensive

The British decided to attack before the Germans had a chance to strike. Their first target was Germany's largest naval base outside Europe, the port of Tsingtao, on the Chinese coast. Here, the German fleet in the Far East, under Admiral Maximilian Graf von Spee, consisted of two large battle cruisers and three smaller ones. The British had a squadron of similar size in Hong Kong, but their ships were older and slower.

In 1902, the British had signed an alliance with Japan, to limit German expansion in the Pacific. Now they called on Japan to put the treaty into action. Seeing the war as a chance to gain land for their empire, the Japanese declared war on Germany on August 23, 1914. The Germans had a number of poorly defended island colonies in the Pacific. These were soon occupied by troops from Australia, New Zealand and Japan.

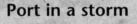

This lithograph shows Japanese soldiers taking part in a night time attack on the German naval base at Tsingtao.

Port in a storm

Tsingtao was heavily fortified and took longer to capture. At the start of September, Japanese ships began bombing the port, and sent 50,000 troops, joined by a small Anglo-Indian force, to attack by land. The defiant German force of just 3,000 marines held out for over two months until they were forced to surrender. Their defeat marked the end of Germany's empire in the Pacific.

Terror at sea

As soon as he heard that Japan was joining the Allies, Spee's fleet fled the Pacific for South America. Meanwhile, one of his captains, Karl von Müller, set off for India, which was part of the British empire. When he shelled Madras, one of India's key trading ports, he sent the financial markets in London into chaos. Müller went on to capture 23 merchant ships, then sank a Russian cruiser and a French destroyer. After two months prowling the oceans, his ship was finally sunk by an Australian ship that was escorting a convoy of troops from Australia and New Zealand to fight in Europe.

The surviving sailors of one of Spee's ships are picked up by British dreadnought HMS *Inflexible* after the Battle of the Falklands.

INTERNET LINK

For a link to a website with photographs of warships and maps showing the biggest naval battles of the First World War, go to **www.usborne-quicklinks.com**

Clash at Coronel

In late October, the Royal Navy intercepted a German radio message, which revealed that Admiral von Spee was on course for the coast of Chile. The nearest British fleet was on patrol off the southern tip of South America. Its commander, Vice-Admiral Sir Christopher Cradock, was ordered to deal with Spee.

The two fleets clashed near the Chilean port of Coronel, on November 1. The British force was outnumbered and outgunned by the Germans. As the sun went down, the British ships were silhouetted on the horizon, making them easy targets. Cradock's flagship, HMS *Good Hope*, and HMS *Monmouth* were sunk, and 1,570 sailors were killed. It was the first time Britain had been defeated at sea for over a century, and there was a public outcry. Desperate to save face, the British sent out two of their newest, most powerful dreadnoughts, *Invincible* and *Inflexible*, with the express purpose of finding Admiral von Spee's fleet and destroying it.

Fighting for the Falklands

The German High Command ordered Graf von Spee to return home. But with the British navy hot on his heels, he knew he would never make it. Instead he resolved to do, "as much mischief as I can, until my ammunition runs out, or until a foe far superior in power succeeds in catching me."

The Royal Navy had a radio communications station in the Falklands. Thinking it was undefended, Spee decided to attack. But this was exactly where *Invincible* and *Inflexible* were taking on fuel. The British counterattacked. Outgunned and low on ammunition, four German cruisers, including Spee's, were sunk. He went down with his ship, and his two sons were among the 2,200 German sailors who drowned. Germany's cruiser war was over.

39

AFRICAN ACTION

In 1914, most of Africa was divided into European colonies, so it wasn't long before the war spread there too. Over two million Africans served in the conflict, making great sacrifices for purely European causes.

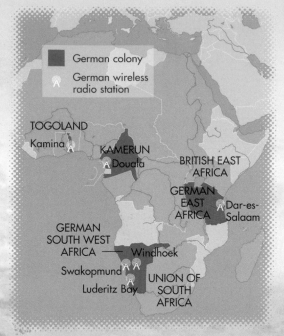

This map shows Germany's African colonies, shaded in red, and their six wireless radio stations.

Coastal targets

From the outset, the Allies' first aim was to capture Germany's African ports and wireless radio stations, to prevent supplies, troops or military orders from getting through. They quickly gained control of Togoland and the coast of Kamerun, but it was an easy start to what soon became a difficult, drawn-out campaign.

Southern rebels

The Union of South Africa was part of the British empire, so joined the Allies, but not without a struggle. The country was divided between British and Dutch settlers (Boers) who had fought a bitter war in 1899-1902, ending in a British victory. The wounds of that defeat were still raw in the memories of many South African Boers. At the start of the war, the South African president, Louis Botha, sent troops to invade German South West Africa. Many Boers in the army refused to take part, and asked the Germans to help them retake South Africa. But the Germans couldn't spare any troops, as they were already vastly outnumbered defending their colony. Botha's war minister, General Jan Smuts, soon put down the Boer rebellion. By July 1915, he had forced Germany to surrender South West Africa.

British African troops from the Gold Coast wade across a river during the campaign in German East Africa.

Bees in the bush

In German East Africa, the British floundered when they came up against the talents of the charismatic German commander, Colonel Paul von Lettow-Vorbeck. Around 8,000 troops were shipped from India to try to seize the colony. In November, 1914, they landed near Tanga, a German port north of Dar-es-Salaam. On the march through dense jungle to Tanga, the Indians were ambushed by von Lettow-Vorbeck's troops. His men were outnumbered, eight to one, but the Indians had no training in bush warfare and were easily overcome. Things got ugly when the fighting roused swarms of angry bees, forcing both sides to flee. Later, it became known as the Battle of the Bees.

40

Undefeated commander

Colonel von Lettow-Vorbeck became something of a legend among friends and enemies alike. After the Battle of the Bees, he invited the British commanders to his lodgings to compare notes over a bottle of brandy. He also arranged for the wounded Indian soldiers to be treated by his medics.

Without radio or naval links to Germany, von Lettow-Vorbeck's men became self-sufficient, growing their own food and raiding enemy stores for guns and ammunition. For the rest of the war, they used guerrilla tactics to play cat-and-mouse with the Allies. They lured them ever deeper into East Africa, but avoided direct combat as much as possible. He was the only military commander to last the entire war without suffering a single defeat.

Colonel von Lettow-Vorbeck (second from the right) enjoys a drink with friends at his lodgings in German East Africa.

The burden of war

Many Africans who volunteered for the army were taken on to work as porters. Africa had few roads or train lines, so equipment, supplies and even officers were all hauled across the continent on men's backs. Porters were given smaller rations than soldiers, and thousands died of malnutrition, exhaustion and disease. Hundreds of thousands of African civilians are estimated to have starved during the war, when harvests failed because the farmers had been marched off to war.

TURKEY ENTERS THE WAR

Just days before the outbreak of war, the Turkish government had signed an alliance with Germany, against Russia. For the first two months, the Turks remained neutral. Then, on October 29, their fleet joined two German warships in an attack on the Russian fleet in the Black Sea. From this point on, Turkey was officially in the war on the side of the Central powers.

The 'sick man' and the Young Turks

In 1914, the Ottoman Turkish empire, ruled by Sultan Mehmed V, was a shadow of its former glory. It was nicknamed the 'sick man of Europe' because it had lost control of many of its former territories and its government was in debt. The Sultan's power was on the wane too. Since 1908, Turkey had effectively been run by a political party known as the Young Turks. Led by a politician named Enver Pasha, they had modernized the Turkish government and its armed forces. They hoped an alliance with Germany would enable them to win back their lost empire too.

Enver Pasha (on the right), leader of the Young Turks, meets his new ally, Kaiser Wilhelm.

INTERNET LINK

For a link to a website with loads of snapshots of everyday life in the Turkish capital, Constantinople, at the outbreak of the war, go to **www.usborne-quicklinks.com**

Oilfield empires

Britain and Turkey both controlled territory around the Persian Gulf. Southern Persia (present-day Iran) had become especially valuable to the British since they had discovered oil there in 1909, and set up the Anglo-Persian Oil Company. It was the Royal Navy's main fuel supplier, and they couldn't afford to risk losing it. Now that the Turks had entered the war, British oil supplies in the Middle East were under threat.

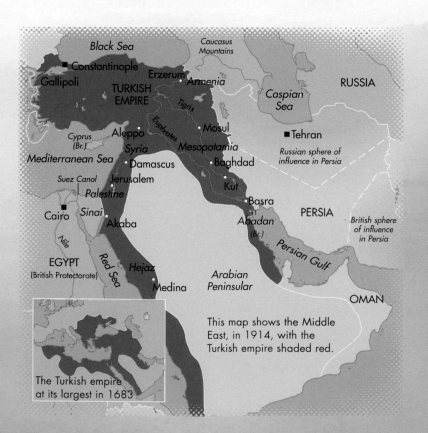

This map shows the Middle East, in 1914, with the Turkish empire shaded red.

The Turkish empire at its largest in 1683

Staff of the Anglo-Persian Oil Company construct one of the region's first oil derricks, in 1909.

Target Basra

The British had already sent Indian troops to guard the oil refinery on the British-held island of Abadan in the Persian Gulf, and the pipeline connecting it to the Persian oilfields. When Turkey declared war, the British government in India decided to invade Turkish Mesopotamia (now Iraq). If they could capture Basra and the surrounding area, they would be able to secure their oil supplies.

Indian troops advanced overland from Abadan into Mesopotamia. At the same time, British naval units sailed up the Euphrates to join them. The combined forces met only weak resistance from the Turks. Within a month, they had occupied Basra.

Indian machine gunners defend the Suez canal against attack from Turkish troops.

Suez

Humiliated by their defeat in Mesopotamia, the Turks were determined to strike back at the Allies. Officially, Egypt was still part of the Ottoman Turkish empire, but it had been under British control since the 1880s. Now the Turks wanted it back. On German advice, Enver Pasha decided to start by attacking the Suez Canal, which the British used to convoy essential supplies and troops from India and Australasia to Europe.

The Turkish army of 25,000 troops set out from Damascus, across the parched sands of the Sinai Desert. Tough soldiers, they were trained to march vast distances in extreme conditions, on very little food. They made the journey without losing a single man. But the Allies were waiting for them. Nine British warships were guarding the canal, and 30,000 British and Indian troops counterattacked with machine-gun fire from the opposite bank. The Turks suffered 1,200 casualties and retreated into the desert.

43

JIHAD AND GENOCIDE

Enver Pasha's determination to take back Turkey's old Empire did not end with Egypt. While his soldiers were marching across the Sinai Desert, he sent more troops north, to the Caucasus Mountains. The region was home to people of many cultures and religions, whose territory had been fought over by Russia and Turkey throughout the last 200 years. Now this wild, mountainous land was to provide the backdrop for one of the biggest human tragedies of the war.

A holy war?

Islam was the official religion of the Ottoman Turkish empire. Two weeks after entering the war, the Sultan declared an Islamic holy war, or *jihad*, against the Allies. In fact, it had been the Kaiser's idea. He hoped that a jihad would inspire Muslims in India and Egypt to rise against the British empire, and knock them out of the war.

But the Sultan's call to holy war was largely ignored, even in Turkey. The Young Turks were driven more by political and territorial aims, than by religion. However, in the Caucasus region, Enver exploited local religious tensions, with horrific consequences.

Battling the elements

In December, 1914, Turkish troops invaded the Caucasus, aiming to ambush the Russians at Sarikamish. Since the Russian defeats at Tannenberg and the Masurian Lakes, much of the Russian army had been transferred to the Eastern Front in Poland, leaving only 60,000 men behind to face the Turks. When they heard that a Turkish army of nearly double that number was advancing rapidly, the Russians began to retreat.

Then the weather turned bad. Temperatures plummeted and blizzards left the Turks stranded. Many of them did not have proper coats, and some were even without boots. On December 29, the Russians launched a counterattack. This resulted in a catastrophic defeat for the Turks, whose ice-clogged artillery failed to fire. They lost over 75,000 men. As many as 30,000 of them are said to have frozen to death before they even met their enemy.

Constantinople – the political and religious heart of the Turkish empire

Exhaustion written on their weary faces, these Armenian people have been forced to trek from their homeland to Aleppo, in Syria.

Unholy massacre

The persecution did not end there. In June 1915, the Turkish government ordered the deportation of all Armenians to Aleppo, in Syria. Fired up with anti-Armenian and anti-Christian feeling, the Turkish army drove them out of their homes, seizing their possessions and raping the women. They were herded across the Syrian Desert, forced to make the 800km (500 miles) journey on foot, without shelter and with little food. Thousands died of exposure, starvation and disease on the way. Many who survived the journey suffered the same fate in squalid prison camps in Aleppo. Altogether, at least 800,000 Armenians died in what is now considered a brutal act of genocide.

Scapegoats

After the disaster, Enver Pasha looked around for someone to blame and he chose the Armenians. They were a Christian minority, living on both sides of the disputed territory. During the conflict, some Armenian soldiers serving in the Turkish army had gone over to the Russian side, hoping to drive out the Turks and declare Armenian independence. In the spring of 1915, all Armenians in the Turkish army were rounded up and sent to work camps, where most of them died.

INTERNET LINK

For a link to a website where you can see photos of Armenian refugees taken by a German officer based in the Ottoman empire during the war, go to **www.usborne-quicklinks.com**

A small number of the many thousands of Armenian children driven from their homes by the Turks

THE EASTERN FRONT

The Eastern Front was the longest battle zone of the war, stretching from the Baltic coast right down to the Black Sea. Fighting here were the three empires of Germany, Austria-Hungary and Russia. Battles took place on an epic scale, with grand sweeping offensives, covering hundreds of miles. This put a great strain on the countries involved, and none of them was able to achieve a clear victory.

The Eastern Front during the early stages of the war. The green line shows the front line where most of the fighting took place.

An ailing empire

The Turkish empire was described as a sick man, but Austria-Hungary was in no fit state to fight a war either. Its vast, sprawling empire, was made up of people of many ethnic groups, including Hungarians, Czechs, Germans, Slavs and Serbs, many of them calling for independence. This meant that the empire was becoming more and more difficult to hold together. Parts of its army could not be trusted to stay loyal in the heat of battle.

Easy target?

As soon as Germany declared war, the Tsar's troops began preparing to invade Austria-Hungary's north eastern province of Galicia. The Russians knew that the Austro-Hungarians would be weak without the help of their allies, so they planned a lightning attack on the Austro-Hungarian frontier, while the Germans were still tied up in France.

Serbian onslaught

The Austro-Hungarians were not only concerned with Russia. Their first priority was to punish Serbia for the murder of Archduke Franz Ferdinand. Their military chief, Franz Conrad, believed the Russians would take 30 days to mobilize their troops. This would give them time to defeat Serbia – or so he thought.

Conrad placed some troops in Galicia, but sent the majority of his army into Serbia. They were told to expect resistance from both soldiers and civilians, and to show no mercy. In the opening days of the war, up to 4,000 Serbian civilians were killed. But their army fought back fiercely. By the end of December 1914, the Serbs had driven the Austro-Hungarians out of their country.

Fortress under fire

While most of the Austro-Hungarian army was fighting in Serbia, the Russians invaded Galicia. They won a crucial victory at Lemberg (now Lvov) in 1914, forcing the Austrians to retreat to the Carpathian Mountains. There, in September, the Russians besieged Przemysl, the fortress town where Conrad had his headquarters. In the spring of 1915, the 120,000 Austrian troops under siege surrendered. The Austrians continued to fight back, but they badly needed help from Germany.

INTERNET LINK
For a link to a website with maps, photographs and film footage of the war on the Eastern Front, go to
www.usborne-quicklinks.com

German troops march into the vast open fields of Galicia, which is now part of Poland.

A great retreat

The Germans could not allow Galicia to fall into Russian hands, as this might leave industrial areas in the east of Germany vulnerable to attack. So in spring, 1915, their troops entered the region. Taken by surprise and low on ammunition, the Russian forces soon collapsed. In what became known as the Great Retreat, the Russians lost hundreds of thousands of men, and the Germans seized control of most of present-day Poland, Lithuania, Belarus, and later, the Ukraine.

After this drastic defeat, Tsar Nicholas sacked his uncle Grand Duke Nicholas, who had been in command of the Russian forces. He decided to do the job himself. This meant that the Tsar would be directly to blame for any military failures or unpopular strategies. It was an ill-judged decision that would later play a part in his downfall.

Communities in peril

Along the Eastern Front, especially in Galicia, the war brought much suffering to the population, which was a fragile patchwork of different racial and religious communities. No minority group was safe: Serbs, Slavs and Jews all suffered persecution at the hands of ransacking armies, occupying powers and old rivals.

From 1915, major cities on both sides were subjected to air attacks. This air raid warden, high above Paris, is sounding a siren to warn people to take shelter before an imminent attack.

1915

DEADLOCK

As the war dragged into a second year, soldiers and civilians had to adjust to the demands of a long-term conflict. Neither side could see a way to break the stalemate on the Western Front. Instead, commanders turned their attentions to other fronts, seeking new allies and using an array of deadly modern weapons, and desperate tactics to try to weaken their opponents.

A DEADLY MIST

After six months of savage fighting on the Western Front, Ypres was still in Allied hands. Allied soldiers occupied a bulge of land around the town which jutted deep into enemy lines. Here, German commanders used a terrifying new weapon to try to break the stalemate.

A ghostly cloud

The bulge was known as the Ypres salient. It was heavily defended with trenches and artillery, and many believed the Germans would never break through. But, at dusk on April 22, 1915, French sentries north of Ypres noticed a ghostly, yellow-green cloud drifting across no-man's-land. They watched in horror as the cloud inched closer and their throats and eyes began to burn in pain. The Germans had opened 6,000 canisters of deadly chlorine gas. Heavier than air, the gas streamed into the Allied trenches, poisoning every hiding place. The French troops ran for cover, screaming and dying as they staggered away.

Drowning men

By releasing this gas, which they first used on the Eastern Front in January that year, the Germans had broken an international agreement. But they weren't the first to use chemical weapons in the war. French gunners had fired tear gas shells at the enemy the previous year. Tear gas caused coughing and sore eyes, but it didn't kill. Chlorine gas burned into a soldier's lungs and throat. The victims eventually 'drowned' on their own body fluids bubbling up from their damaged lungs. It was an agonizing way to die.

Until they developed more effective protection against gas, many soldiers had to improvise. These Scottish troops are using goggles and cotton masks.

A line of British soldiers, blinded in a gas attack, awaits medical attention. Each man clutches the shoulder of the man in front for support.

Forewarnings

German soldiers taken prisoner by the Allies had revealed the German plan to use gas, but these warnings were ignored. Some British generals thought gas couldn't be used as part of an organized attack, as it relied too much on the direction of the wind. But the new weapon had a devastating effect at Ypres. German infantry stormed through the 6km (4 miles) gap left in the line by the retreating French soldiers. By nightfall the Germans were only 3km (2 miles) from Ypres and had started digging in.

This German soldier wears a more sophisticated gas mask than the ones on the opposite page. His horses have been provided with their own gas masks too.

Fighting back

The German raiders wore cloth masks over their faces, to protect their eyes and filter gas out of the air they breathed. But the Allies quickly discovered how to make simple gas masks too. Chlorine dissolves in water, so if a soldier breathed though a wet cloth he was safe. Canadian and British troops wore rag masks over their faces and fought hard to defend their trenches.

The experiment fails

The Second Battle of Ypres, as it became known, raged on until the end of May. The Germans gained some ground, but they hadn't been prepared for the success of their attack. If they had had enough men they might have captured the whole salient and cracked the Western Front. But they ran out of troops and supplies before they could seize Ypres. The gas attack shocked the world, but Allied forces quickly began to use their own chemical weapons too. More effective gas masks were invented and soldiers gradually learned how to deal with this new horror. Gas just became one more hazard in a brutal and unrelenting war.

SETTLING IN

By the summer of 1915, there were four million soldiers eating, sleeping and dying in the trenches. Despite all its hardships, the men adapted quickly to their new life below the surface. The bulk of their time was spent preparing for attacks, taking turns at sentry duty – and digging. But they still tried to find a few minutes in the day when they could rest, joke and try to recreate some of the lost comforts of home.

In this cartoon from a postcard, French soldiers have set up a decoy for the enemy to shoot at while they play cards.

A nervous dawn

Armies work to timetables and routines, and trench duty was no exception. The men were awake before first light, preparing for *Stand-to*, the order to be ready with loaded weapons. Poor visibility at dawn and dusk made it hard to spot attacks, so soldiers climbed onto the firestep, a platform cut into the trench wall, to peer into no-man's-land. Some men called this the morning hate, when both sides exchanged a few warning shots and shouts. Others remarked on the beauty of the morning skies and the eerie quiet of no-man's-land.

A waiting game

In the daylight hours, it was too dangerous to move around in the open, so men cleaned their weapons, did their chores and tried to rest. If a soldier was a talented marksman, he might be chosen as a sniper, picking off enemy soldiers by aiming his rifle through a steel shutter in the parapet. But even a sniper's life was precarious – bullets could puncture steel plate, and every inch of the trenches was watched with periscopes and mirrors.

Forced to spend months away from home, soldiers found all kinds of ways to relieve the boredom and to keep morale up. These Canadian troops and their pantomime horse are rehearsing for a show.

Night raiding

Under the cover of darkness, soldiers slipped into no-man's-land to do things that were impossible in daylight, such as laying and repairing barbed wire. They kept total silence, muffling any tools with cloths and using hand signals to communicate. Units with special combat training went out on raids, to try to capture a prisoner who could tell them about the enemy's plans. Squads sent into no-man's-land, to recover their dead and wounded, could suddenly be lit up by flares and shot at by enemy machine gunners.

Creature comforts

In the reserve trenches, soldiers had more spare time. They held shooting contests, scavenged for weapons in old sections of the battlefield and wrote letters home. By cutting into the trench walls, they created small rooms called dugouts, furnished with beds, tables and chairs, and even electric lights and gramophone records. Postal services brought newspapers and food packages, as well as letters from home and, for the better-off soldiers, brandy and cigars. Even with all these distractions, many soldiers still found time to write and print their own unofficial front-line magazines, where they shared their experiences and poked fun at army life.

These French officers may be in a trench near the front line, but they are dining in style and even have a vase of flowers on the table.

INTERNET LINK
For a link to a website where you can find out more about life in the trenches, go to www.usborne-quicklinks.com

Fine dining

Officers and men served together in the trench, but behind the lines they went their separate ways. Privates (low-ranking soldiers) and junior officers enjoyed hot food and a bottle of wine in the rest areas, while senior officers could take rides on their horses or go off on shooting parties. Some generals lived almost like kings, sleeping in grand country houses and controlling their armies from way behind the lines. The French commander, General Joffre, even insisted on taking a two-hour lunch every afternoon. It's not surprising that some soldiers were suspicious of their commanders and the way they were directing the war.

A DANGEROUS VOYAGE

By May 1915, Germany's submarine blockade around Britain was causing a serious shortage of food and raw materials. U-boat crews had clear orders: sink anything that might be carrying troops or supplies to the enemy. But some captains of non-military ships thought they were safe from attack, and calmly set sail into dangerous waters.

An ocean greyhound

The British ocean liner *Lusitania* was one of the world's fastest and most elegant passenger ships. Her best cabins offered every luxury and she could carry almost 2,000 passengers and crew on her six-day Atlantic crossing.

On May 1, 1915, the ship left New York, bound for Liverpool. A few passengers were alarmed by announcements they'd read in the morning newspapers, paid for by the German Embassy, warning them not to sail into the submarine 'war zone' around Britain. But the ship's captain, William Turner, saw no cause for concern. He didn't believe the Germans would dare to attack an ocean liner as large and as famous as the *Lusitania*. And even with six of its 25 boilers shut down because of wartime coal shortages, he thought his ship could easily outpace a prowling U-boat.

The *Lusitania* leaves New York for the last time. Just a week later, the liner had been sunk.

Predator and prey

Five days into the voyage, Turner received a telegram from Royal Navy headquarters. U-boat *U-20* had just sunk two merchant ships, south of Ireland. On May 7, the *Lusitania* arrived in these same waters, lost in a thick fog. When the fog cleared, Turner turned ashore to fix his position by sighting a landmark. Little did he know, he was being watched through a U-boat periscope.

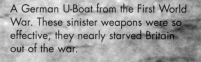

A German U-Boat from the First World War. These sinister weapons were so effective, they nearly starved Britain out of the war.

Torpedo away

Inside submarine *U-20*, Kapitan-leutnant Walther Schwieger couldn't believe his luck. He'd already spotted a 'forest of masts' on the horizon and realized a huge British ship was approaching. But the target was too far away and moving too quickly. Suddenly, the ship altered course and headed straight for the U-boat. Not hesitating for a second, Schwieger sent a torpedo hissing through the choppy sea.

Shock waves

The torpedo ripped into the liner's front cargo hold and exploded. Seconds later, another explosion, more powerful than the first, tore through the ship. The *Lusitania* rolled sideways, throwing passengers off their feet and sending lifeboats crashing into the waves. It took only 18 minutes for the mighty liner to sink to the bottom, with the loss of 1,198 lives.

Schwieger always said he was amazed that a single torpedo had destroyed the ship. He thought there would be time for the passengers to climb into lifeboats and escape before the liner sank. But his attack without warning sparked international fury and anti-German riots across Britain and the US. Most damaging of all, it led some leading American politicians to accuse the Germans of piracy, and to call for the United States to join the war.

Secret cargo

With over 120 American citizens drowned, US President Woodrow Wilson was forced to act. He sent the German government a series of strongly-worded protest notes, demanding an immediate end to submarine warfare. In response, the Germans tried to justify the sinking by accusing the British of transporting munitions inside passenger ships. The *Lusitania* had indeed been loaded with crates of bullets and shell parts, but there was no proof that these had caused the massive second explosion – as the Germans claimed. A recent theory suggests it might have been caused by an exploding boiler.

While diplomats argued, public opinion in America began to harden against Germany. All around the United States, people began to ask themselves how much longer they could avoid being drawn in to this destructive global war.

INTERNET LINK

For a link to a website with photographs and paintings of the *Lusitania*, and to read the stories of some of the victims and survivors of the sinking, go to **www.usborne-quicklinks.com**

The destruction of the *Lusitania* caused outrage around the world. This is the cover of a French book, which describes the sinking of the liner as a crime.

OUT OF THIN AIR

While fighting on land and sea raged on, generals looked skyward for fresh ways to attack the enemy. They ordered aircraft designers to make bigger and more powerful planes to carry bombs. And the Germans sent a formidable new invention lumbering across the skies. It was called the zeppelin.

Count Ferdinand von Zeppelin, who spent his entire fortune developing his airships

Flying cigars

The zeppelin was the brainchild of a retired German general – Count Ferdinand von Zeppelin. As a young military cadet he'd been fascinated by the observation balloons used by artillery teams to check their shots. Zeppelin calculated that by fixing engines and steering controls to balloons he could produce a fleet of 'airships' fit to rule the skies.

In the early 1900s, dozens of inventors were working on airship designs, but Zeppelin's was one of the best. His was tube-shaped and as long as a battleship. Instead of relying on a single balloon to lift it off the ground, it boasted over a dozen huge sacks of hydrogen gas inside a skeleton of metal hoops, covered in tough fabric. Three propellers moved it through the air and it was powerful enough to carry passengers – and high explosive bombs.

Look out below

The German navy began using zeppelins for reconnaissance patrols above the North Sea. Then, during the first months of the war, they were used to bomb the Belgian forts of Liège and Antwerp. At first, some German politicians had their doubts about using zeppelins as bombers because they were very expensive to build. But, in January 1915, the Kaiser gave the order for zeppelins to be sent to attack British towns.

Into thin air

On January 13, 1915, a pair of zeppelins bombed the east coast of England, killing four people. This was the first of over fifty air raids carried out over Britain that year. There were zeppelin raids on Paris too. This was partly in response to French air raids on German cities. Blackouts were enforced in many places, making it difficult for the zeppelin pilots to spot their targets. The menacing bulk and droning growl of the airship soon earned it a fearsome reputation, inspiring dread among the civilians cowering in the darkness below.

Taking the flak

Zeppelins cruised at very high altitudes, usually beyond the range of artillery gunners on the ground. But if an airship was hit, the shell passed straight through it. Leaking gas slowly, the zeppelin had plenty of time to limp home for repairs. Some pilots were so desperate to hit back at the airships they flew to dangerous heights to attack them from above with light bombs or grenades. But by early 1916, British fighter planes were armed with a new kind of 'incendiary' bullet that set fire to the gas in the airships, sending them up in flames.

Zeppelin *LZ77* takes off in Germany. It raided eastern England in 1915 and was shot down in France the following year.

INTERNET LINK

For a link to a website with facts, figures, photographs and diagrams of zeppelins or to find out what life was like during the air raids, go to **www.usborne-quicklinks.com**

British officials inspect the skeletal remains of zeppelin *L33*, which was shot down in September, 1916.

Angry giants

Next, Zeppelin built a new airship that could fly higher than the fighters, but the German military was already developing a new weapon – the Gotha bomber. In June 1917, a group of these huge planes swarmed over London, pounding the city and killing 162 people. Gothas were fast and well armed, but British designers quickly produced planes to fight back with even greater firepower. The zeppelins and heavy bombers were menacing symbols of the air war, but the air raids did little to affect the eventual outcome of the war.

THE HOME FRONT

With civilians living under the threat of bombardment and dealing with shortages caused by naval blockades, the First World War had a greater impact on people's everyday lives than any previous conflict. While the men were away fighting, it was up to the people left behind to keep the 'home front' running smoothly.

The Germans came up with clever ways to get around shortages on the home front. This poster asks people to save their fruit stones and take them to government collection points so the nut oil can be turned into fuel.

Women into work

Many women had worked before the war, but the jobs available to them then were limited, and most were expected to stay at home to look after the family. In the early part of the war, women were mainly involved in charity work or making bandages, socks and balaclavas to send to the trenches. But as more and more men left for the front, women had to take their places.

The war created new jobs too, keeping the armed forces supplied with munitions, food and equipment. Governments used propaganda posters to persuade women of all ages and classes that it was their duty to work for the war. Millions answered the call. They operated telephone exchanges, drove buses, worked in agriculture and even took on dangerous and heavy jobs such as mining, shipbuilding and packing explosive shells.

The politics of war

In most countries, rival political groups agreed to put aside their differences to focus on winning the war. Governments were reorganized so members of different parties could work together in what is called a coalition government. They brought in tough measures to control industrial production and wages, and to prevent workers from striking.

Before the war, most women weren't allowed to take part in elections. In Britain, women known as Suffragettes had spent decades fighting for the right to vote. Their leader, Emmeline Pankhurst, suspended the 'Votes for Women' campaign to encourage women to support the war. Eventually this would further their cause. In the General Election of December 1918, British women over 30 were granted the vote for the first time, partly in recognition of their wartime efforts.

INTERNET LINK

For links to websites where you can find out more about life on the Home Front and see more propaganda posters, go to **www.usborne-quicklinks.com**

These Welsh women are hauling clay to a factory where it will be made into bricks.

War and want

Even with women replacing male farm workers, most countries experienced food shortages at some point. Everywhere, posters and leaflets advised people not to be wasteful. Everyone had to get used to waiting in line for food when it became available. Rationing was introduced in Germany, and later, in Britain too. But, as goods became scarce, prices rose faster than people's wages and many struggled to afford even the basics. Britain and France got over the problem by fixing prices, but in Germany, Austria-Hungary and Russia, the shortages were much worse and thousands of civilians suffered terrible poverty and malnutrition.

Hard times and good times

Many people who lived in the combat zones were forced to flee their war-ravaged homes. Some were able to stay with relatives, but many had to escape their countries and take shelter in refugee camps. They were clothed, fed and given medical care by local charity workers, but their lodgings were often very basic.

Even for those who didn't face such traumatic upheaval, it was important to keep up morale. Paris was not far from the Western Front, so many soldiers visited the city on leave. To entertain the troops, many cafés, cabaret bars, cinemas and galleries stayed open throughout the war.

This munition factory worker – or 'munitionette' as they were called – is checking and packing shells to send to the front.

"It is my painful duty..."

While everyone on the Home Front tried to keep business running as usual, they dreaded hearing the news of the death of a loved one. People anxiously scoured daily casualty lists, published in the newspapers, to find out whether anyone they knew was dead, missing or wounded. Official notices that men had been killed in action opened with the words, "It is my painful duty to inform you..." and were usually sent to the soldiers' relatives by telegram. For the millions of women and children who read these harrowing words, normal family life would never be the same.

GALLIPOLI

For the British and imperial forces, Gallipoli was the most disastrous campaign of 1915. Their plan had been to capture the Dardanelles Straits and the Gallipoli peninsula from Turkey, then to storm Constantinople. But the operation was doomed from the start, by poor leadership and bad planning. The men who served in Gallipoli endured appalling conditions as they fought a hopeless battle through nine bitter months.

This German cartoon shows Turkey as a man sweeping the Allies from his shore.

Churchill's plan

When the Turks entered the war, they blocked the Dardanelles Straits to all enemy ships. This cut off the Russians from their allies and trapped most of their fleet in the Black Sea. Already fully stretched by the war in Galicia and the Caucasus, they asked Britain for help.

Winston Churchill, the future British prime minister, was the First Lord of the Admiralty, in charge of the Royal Navy. He was convinced that if they could push through the Dardanelles, Allied naval forces would be able to capture Constantinople, forcing the Turks to surrender.

Deadly straits

Putting Churchill's plan into action wasn't going to be easy. The Dardanelles were laid with mines, and the cliffs overlooking the water were lined with guns and forts. In February 1915, the Allies bombarded the forts at the mouth of the straits, ready to steam in. On March 18, an Anglo-French armada of 16 battleships thrust into the narrow straits. A French ship and two British ones struck undetected mines and sank, and three more ships were badly damaged. The fleet was withdrawn and minesweepers were sent in to clear the way. But heavy shelling from the shore made this impossible. So, the British decided to send land forces to try to capture the Gallipoli Peninsula, instead.

Blood on the beaches

On April 25, 35,000 Allied troops went ashore at Cape Helles, and 17,000 men from the Australian and New Zealand Army Corps (Anzacs) landed on the west coast. Neither landing went to plan. The Anzacs landed in the wrong place: a narrow beach, hemmed in by steep hills (later known as Anzac Cove). Before they could clamber out of the cove, the Turks opened fire on them from trenches in the high ridges above. Further south, at Cape Helles, soldiers were shot down before they even reached the shore. The sea is said to have turned red with their blood.

The Allies had no choice but to push forward. But they didn't get far. The Turks, fighting to save their country, put up a strong resistance. Soon, both sides were digging in for trench warfare. In August, the Allies sent in reinforcements, landing at Suvla Bay, but they still failed to break the deadlock.

Flies, thirst and frostbite

It wasn't just enemy soldiers the men in Gallipoli were fighting. As spring turned to summer, the intense heat became almost unbearable, and drinking water grew scarce. The corpses rotting in no-man's-land, now buzzing with flies, began to reek. The flies contaminated the soldiers' food, infected their wounds and spread diseases. Dysentery raged through the trenches. Then the harsh winter set in. The numbers of sick soldiers soared, with men suffering from both frostbite and pneumonia.

INTERNET LINK

For a link to a website with eyewitness accounts and images of events at Gallipoli, go to www.usborne-quicklinks.com

Bayonets at the ready, Anzac troops scramble uphill to attack the Turkish front line.

The battlegrounds of Gallipoli. Shown here are the Allied landing zones and the deadly Dardanelles Straits.

Costly victory

In November, the Allies decided to withdraw their troops, and by January 9, 1916, the last of them had left. They had lost nearly 50,000 men, most from disease, and they had absolutely nothing to show for it. Churchill had already resigned as a result of the fiasco, and the British government was replaced by a new coalition, soon to be led by a new prime minister, David Lloyd George. The people of Constantinople celebrated their proud victory. But it had come at a terrible price: more than 87,000 Turks died defending Gallipoli and their remaining army was in tatters.

Antipodean pride

Gallipoli was the Anzacs' first major action of the war and they had fought with great determination. A third of those who took part in the landings died. Many Anzacs were British-born and proud to fight for Britain. But they returned home with a strong sense of their own distinct national identities. Gallipoli earned a special place in the history of Australia and New Zealand. Every year people remember their war dead on April 25, which is named Anzac Day.

61

WAR IN THE SNOW

While sun-scorched armies were slogging it out in Gallipoli, two more countries were gearing up to throw themselves into the line of fire. Italy and Bulgaria had been sitting on the sidelines since the start of the war. In 1915, the two countries finally declared their allegiances and entered the conflict on opposing sides.

Italian soldiers hoist a heavy field gun up a steep snow-bound cliff.

'Sacro egoismo'

When the war broke out, Italy declared its neutrality, although it was technically allied to the Central Powers. But the Italian prime minister, Antonio Salandra, secretly negotiated with both sides to see which would make him the better offer. He called this policy *sacro egoismo* (or 'sacred self-interest'). On April 26, 1915, Italy joined the Allied Powers. In return, they were promised control of Italian-speaking areas of Austria-Hungary and other territories, if the Allies won the war.

Uphill battles

The Italians declared war against Austria-Hungary (but not Germany) on May 23. They immediately launched attacks along the whole of the frontier, most of which ran through the Alps. The Austrians retreated a short way, but only to dig trenches on higher ground. This gave them a tactical advantage over their attackers. Bitter fighting took place along the Isonzo River on the eastern section of the Front. By the end of 1915, the Italians had fought four battles to try to take control of the river. But they suffered over 300,000 casualties and barely gained an inch of territory.

Soldiers on skis

The Alpine terrain of the Italian Front was possibly the toughest battleground of the whole war. Battling dizzying high altitudes, heavy snowfalls and frequent avalanches, the two armies dug trenches into the jagged peaks of the Alps. Both sides used specialist troops, trained in rock climbing and skiing. They had to develop ingenious engineering techniques to haul heavy artillery and supplies up the sheer rock faces and glaciers. During the war, around 650,000 soldiers lost their lives on the Italian Front. In the winter of 1915-16 alone, about 100,000 men died in avalanches.

INTERNET LINK

For a link to a website with a slide show exploring the dangerous and varied landscape of the Italian Front, go to **www.usborne-quicklinks.com**

Burdened with supplies, and equipped with skis, Italian soldiers weave their way up a precarious path along their Alpine frontier.

Bulgaria does a deal

Like Italy, the Bulgarian government chose the side that made the highest bid for their support. With recent successes in Galicia and the Dardanelles, the Central Powers seemed close to winning. So when they promised the Bulgarians control of southern Serbia, they jumped at it. The deal was sealed in September 1915. Within weeks, Bulgaria and Austria-Hungary began a mass assault on Serbia, on two fronts.

Retreat, but no surrender

Serbian troops had successfully fought off the Austro-Hungarian invasion at the start of the war, but the effort had left them exhausted. Hopelessly outnumbered and low on munitions, they begged their allies for support. On October 5, British and French forces landed at the Greek port of Salonika. But, with Bulgarian troops in force on the frontier, the Allies couldn't get through. Four days later, the Austrians took the Serb capital, Belgrade.

Fearing brutality at the hands of these occupying forces, the Serbian army, their king, Peter I, and thousands of civilians fled across the mountains to Albania. Most made the arduous journey on foot. King Peter survived, but over 94,000 soldiers and an unknown number of civilians died of cold and hunger on the way. As a result, Serbia suffered a higher casualty rate (as a percentage of the population) than any other country in the war.

About 155,000 Serbs made it safely to Albania, then sailed to refugee camps in Corfu. Still, they would not give in. As soon as they recovered their strength, 80,000 Serbian soldiers joined the Allies at Salonika, determined to liberate their country. They faced a difficult struggle. The armies on both sides dug trenches and settled in for a long, hard battle for control of southeast Europe.

This map shows the Balkans and the Italian Front on the Alpine border between Italy and Austria-Hungary.

This dramatic picture captures the instant a French soldier is shot. It is from a French movie about the Battle of Verdun, made in 1928 with actors who fought in the war and filmed on the sites where the battles took place.

THE BIG BATTLES

By the end of 1915, military commanders on both sides decided that the only way to break the stalemate in the trenches was to launch their biggest battles yet, in the year ahead. Allied Generals met at Chantilly, in France, where they planned simultaneous attacks on all fronts in the summer of 1916, with a major offensive on the Western Front near the Somme river. But the German high commander, General Falkenhayn, had plans of his own. He aimed to attack the French at Verdun in February. He hoped that this would "bleed France white" and force the Allies to surrender.

Neither of these grand schemes would go according to plan, but 1916 saw a series of huge battles, all relying on the same brutal tactic: slaughter on a vast scale.

THE MINCING MACHINE

In February 1916, a German army of a million men attacked the ancient French city of Verdun. Germany's commanders weren't trying to capture Allied territory or punch a hole in the Western Front. Instead, they were trying to draw the French forces into a long and bloody battle, to grind them down to the last man.

By the end of the siege of Verdun, the ancient fortress city was in ruins.

A numbers game

The German commander, General Erich von Falkenhayn, believed the war had to be won on the Western Front, and he was convinced that, if his troops could crush the French, the other Allies would be forced to make peace. Falkenhayn knew that French troops had strict orders never to give up land to the enemy, so he looked for a weak spot in their line – somewhere dangerous and difficult to defend. Sitting on a salient in the Western Front, Verdun was exposed to German guns on three sides. Since Roman times it had been protected by a ring of stone forts. But these were crumbling and neglected because the French thought they would be useless in modern war. For supplies, the city and its 200,000 defenders relied on a few shell-blasted roads, whereas the Germans had a rail depot just behind their line.

Falkenhayn made the Kaiser a chilling promise. For every dead German at Verdun, three Allied soldiers would be killed. The battle would blaze like a forest fire until the whole French army had been drawn in and consumed.

Closing in

The German attack began with a massive, thousand-gun artillery barrage. German troops surged forward as soon as the shelling lifted, using flamethrowers to drive any surviving defenders out of their trenches. The French fought bravely, but on the third day, the Germans were just a few miles from the city walls.

Road warriors

In desperation, French generals appointed a new commander, General Philippe Pétain, to save Verdun. He worked around the clock to improve his artillery, demanding bigger and better guns, and he used thousands of trucks to bring supplies into the city. They called the road *La Voie Sacrée* – the Sacred Way. Keeping it open became a patriotic mission for the French army.

INTERNET LINK

For a link to a website where you can take a virtual tour of modern-day Verdun, where the battlefields are still strewn with the debris of war, go to **www.usborne-quicklinks.com**

La Voie Sacrée, April 1916. By June, the road was flowing at full capacity, with 12,000 vehicles passing along it every day.

The tide turns

Through March, April and May, the Germans struggled to break French resistance. But their troops were torn to pieces by Pétain's artillery. Verdun was slowly turning into a death-trap for the attackers, with slaughter so shocking, soldiers compared it to a mincing machine. Pounded by millions of shells, the battlefield had become a featureless plain of churned mud and broken bodies. Fighting finally stopped in early December, with the French recapturing their lost ground. Both sides had suffered equally. Over a million men were dead, missing or wounded.

Falkenhayn had underestimated just how savage the fight for Verdun would be. The Kaiser was disappointed and, in August, he appointed two new, aggressive commanders to lead the German military: Field Marshal Paul von Hindenburg and General Erich von Ludendorff.

DREADNOUGHTS DUEL

After two years of small raids in the North Sea, the British and German fleets finally met head-on at the Battle of Jutland. In the largest steel-ship battle ever seen, there was an awesome display of firepower. But when the smoke cleared over the waves, both sides claimed a victory.

Beatty's flagship, HMS *Lion* (left) is hit by German shells and battle cruiser HMS *Queen Mary* is blown up at Jutland.

Sail out and fight

Battles always reflect the character of the commanders who plan and fight them and Jutland was no exception. In January 1916, Admiral Reinhard Scheer took charge of the German High Seas Fleet. Scheer thought his navy had been too timid in its attacks on the British Grand Fleet. So, he ordered his captains to be more aggressive and daring. In May 1916, he took the whole fleet out to sea, hunting for British patrols.

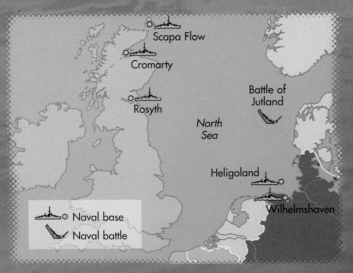

This map shows the British and German naval bases in the North Sea, and the site of the Battle of Jutland.

Jellicoe's choices

In the afternoon of May 30, 1916, British Royal Navy codebreakers passed an urgent message to their commander-in-chief, Admiral John Jellicoe. They had picked up Scheer's radio signals and decoded them using captured German codebooks. They knew exactly what Admiral Scheer was planning.

Jellicoe had to make a difficult decision fast. He desperately wanted to smash the rival fleet, but he had the heavy responsibility of maintaining British naval superiority in the North Sea. If he lost a dozen ships in a submarine attack or unlucky battle, the British sea blockade would collapse and Britain might even lose the war. Despite this, Jellicoe decided to fight.

INTERNET LINK

For links to websites where you can see a gallery of photographs of the Battle of Jutland, and listen to an account of the sinking of the HMS *Indefatigable*, go to **www.usborne-quicklinks.com**

Enemy sighted

Jellicoe set out with the Grand Fleet from the naval base at Scapa Flow, in Orkney, on 31 May. At the same time, a scouting party of six battle cruisers left the port of Rosyth, under the command of Admiral Beatty. When Beatty spotted two small German ships he gave chase. What he didn't know, was that five enemy battle cruisers were waiting just over the horizon.

For the next hour, both sides battered each other with massive shells. Two of Beatty's battle cruisers were sunk and his own flagship was soon belching smoke and flames. But he didn't break off his attack until he sighted the High Seas Fleet rushing in his direction. He immediately turned his ships north, hoping to draw the Germans to Jellicoe's dreadnoughts.

Shortly before the Battle of Jutland, Jellicoe's fleet cruises the North Sea in a formation of six columns. For the battle itself, the British battleships would move into a single line to face their opponents.

Battling it out

The two fleets were hurtling at each other on a collision course. Jellicoe's armada was almost twice as powerful as Scheer's, with 28 dreadnoughts facing the Germans' 16. But tactics and luck would play a large part in the battle ahead.

With only two hours of daylight left, Jellicoe finally spotted the German dreadnoughts and gave the order to fire. But it was the startled Germans who had the first success, as their shells tore into the British battle cruiser HMS *Invincible*. Not wanting to push his luck, Scheer turned his entire fleet under cover of a thick smoke screen. He made a run back to port, thinking he could sneak past the British as they steamed to Heligoland. But the Grand Fleet intercepted his line of ships and scored several hits before Scheer turned again, leaving a 'suicide squad' of old battleships and torpedo ships to protect his rear.

Fearing a massive torpedo attack, which would inflict serious damage on his fleet, Jellicoe held his ships back. By the time he finally decided it was safe to give chase, the German dreadnoughts had slipped away.

Winners and losers

Scheer immediately declared a great German triumph. His fleet had sunk three Royal navy battle cruisers and 12 other ships, at the cost of a single battle cruiser and 10 other German ships. But it was a hollow victory. Jellicoe was criticized for being too cautious, but he had seen off the German fleet and protected his superiority in numbers. The British still ruled the North Sea.

DOOMED YOUTH

Boy Seaman John Cornwell was only 16 years old when he fought at Jutland. He won his country's highest medal for bravery – the Victoria Cross – and the British press called him a hero. But Cornwell was just one of thousands of young soldiers throughout Europe who risked their lives in the war. As many as 15% of all British and German troops were said to be younger than 19 years old.

John Cornwell, won the Victoria Cross medal for his bravery.

One big adventure

Like most people at the time, Cornwell left school at 14. He was working as a delivery boy when the war started. His father went to France with the army but Cornwell had always dreamed of becoming a sailor. Going to sea must have seemed like a great adventure to him. He was only 15 years old when he presented himself at a navy recruitment office. To join the army you had to be 18 – 19 if you wanted to fight overseas – but the navy had a long tradition of recruiting younger boys.

When Cornwell finished his training, he joined a gun team onboard HMS *Chester* and within a few months he found himself in the thick of it, fighting at Jutland. An explosion killed the rest of his team and wounded Cornwell – but he stayed at his post beside the gun, fighting on. His ship returned to port and Cornwell was rushed to the hospital, where he died the following day. His sense of patriotic duty and self-sacrifice impressed the public, who turned out for his funeral procession in droves.

Proof of age

Many boys from poor families were tempted to volunteer by the army's promise of regular food and pay. Instead of seeking foreign adventure, they saw a chance to escape the misery of the slums. Recruitment officers didn't always ask for identification, so many boys simply lied about their age. One British 16-year-old tried to volunteer and made the mistake of saying he was 18. The officer smiled and told him to come back the following morning and see if he was 19.

The British army didn't introduce conscription until 1916, but during the last year of the war, many conscripts, like these boys, were very young.

Classroom heroes

Germany had a huge, conscripted army and didn't actively recruit young boys until late in the war. But, even so, whole classes of them signed up in 1914 to prove their loyalty to the Kaiser. Thousands of young soldiers, aged between 16 and 20, died in the carnage of the First Battle of Ypres. The loss of so many young men shocked the German public. Mourning parents called the battle the Massacre of the Innocents.

Fighting to the death

For many young soldiers, the hardships of trench life were too much, no matter how physically tough they thought they were. One Australian lad, Jim Martin, signed up when his father was turned away for being too short. He was just 14 years old when he sailed for Gallipoli with the Australian army. Martin was big for his age and his farm job had made him strong. But he died of disease and exhaustion after weeks of hard fighting.

The war's horrors spared nobody, neither the brave nor the young. Boys fought and died alongside old soldiers, as countries sent their male populations into the furnace of war.

INTERNET LINK

For a link to a website where you can read about the experiences of boy soldiers of the First World War, go to www.usborne-quicklinks.com

SKY FIGHTERS

Aircraft design was still in its early stages when war flashed across Europe. But planes quickly evolved from lumbering machines into agile fighters. Each tiny improvement in speed or firepower gave pilots a deadly advantage in the battle for the skies.

This is a replica of a British plane, the Bristol Scout. Based on a pre war racing plane, and mounted with a machine gun, it was the first fighter plane to be produced in England in large quantities.

A problem with propellers

As soon as fighting started, both sides used unarmed scout planes to spy on enemy positions. When two rival pilots met in the sky, they simply waved or took potshots at each other with their pistols. Designers soon realized that a plane fitted with machine guns could win battles in the sky.

The best position for a gun was pointing straight ahead, but on most planes the propeller got in the way. In early 1915, an ingenious French pilot named Roland Garros got around this problem by fixing steel deflectors to his propeller blades. If a bullet hit a blade, it would bounce off the deflector towards its target. Garros shot down several enemy pilots before his plane was captured.

A Dutch designer

The Germans ordered the Dutch designer Anthony Fokker to examine and copy the deflectors. But he came up with something better – synchronization gear. This was a system of rods and levers that fired a machine gun only when there was a gap for the bullets to pass between the propeller blades. Fokker installed the gear in his Eindecker monoplane – a single-wing aircraft – to create the first proper fighter plane.

INTERNET LINK

For links to websites where you can find out more about the Red Baron and other flying aces of the First World War, and see photographs of different kinds of aircraft, go to **www.usborne-quicklinks.com**

72

Fokker fodder

Throughout the winter of 1915 the Allies were losing two or three planes a day to Eindeckers. British newspapers called this phase of the war the Fokker Scourge. Allied casualties were so great, British pilots jokingly described their Royal Flying Corps (RFC) as the Suicide Club. But during the Battle of Verdun, the Allies improved their tactics and their planes, and won back control of the skies. One French squadron, known as the Storks, even became famous for their fighter 'aces' – pilots who had shot down five or more enemy aircraft.

It wasn't until early 1917 that new machines once again gave the Germans the upper hand. In April of that year, the RFC lost 245 planes to German fighter pilots, among them the war's greatest ace – Manfred Baron von Richthofen – better known as the Red Baron.

The Germans built about 300 Fokker Dr. I triplanes like this modern replica. A triplane is a plane with three wings.

This photograph of Manfred von Richthofen, the Red Baron, captures some of the young pilot's unswerving determination.

Ace of aces

Every country from Australia to Russia had its aces, usually presented as dashing daredevils in the popular press. The American Edward Rickenbacker notched up 26 kills in just a few, frenzied months of 1918. Frenchman Georges Guynemer became a newspaper celebrity with his 53 victories and was mobbed in the streets by his fans. But Richthofen's incredible record of 80 confirmed kills must earn him the title Ace of Aces.

Knights of the air

Although fighter pilots began flying in larger groups as the war progressed, most air combat came down to one-on-one shootouts known as dogfights. Planes sometimes broke apart as the pilots dived and climbed, and fire was always a risk. French and German pilots were equipped with parachutes, but British flyers weren't. Parachutes were considered too bulky and heavy and some generals thought pilots would be tempted to jump at the first sign of danger.

A flying circus

Richthofen was a skilled hunter and he used his knowledge of stalking and surprise to destroy 80 Allied aircraft. He earned his nickname after painting his plane blood red – a brazen coat of arms that terrified inexperienced pilots. Other German flyers followed the Baron's example, decorating their planes with bright paints. This led Allied soldiers to nickname them the Flying Circus.

Safety in numbers

In the winter of 1917, the tide turned yet again in the air war, as German factories struggled to keep pace with Allied aircraft production. New planes such as the British Sopwith Camel had impressive power and agility compared to the German machines. Richthofen was chasing one of these fighters when he was shot down and killed in early 1918. His Flying Circus was soon outnumbered and decimated. By the end of the war, the Allies were the masters of the sky.

SLAUGHTER AND SACRIFICE

Hoping to divert German troops and supplies from the bloodbath at Verdun, British commanders launched a massive offensive on the Western Front, near the Somme river. After shelling the German trenches for seven days and nights, they expected a quick breakthrough. But the opening hours of the attack were the bloodiest of the entire war.

Moments before going over the top, soldiers attach bayonets to their rifles, ready to advance.

The Big Push

The German line at the Somme was guarded by trenches, miles of barbed wire and hundreds of concrete machine-gun posts. Underground bunkers protected soldiers from even the heaviest shells. But British generals were confident that nothing could stand in the way of what they called their Big Push. They thought that colossal firepower would be able to smash through any obstacle.

An opening barrage of two million shells ripped into the German trenches from above. Below ground, the British planted 21 huge mines, in tunnels they had been digging secretly for months. The mines were timed to explode the moment the barrage lifted. Then, the plan was to send over a wave of infantry to capture any survivors, and to clear the way for the cavalry to charge deep into German territory.

God and the cavalry

In charge of the offensive was Sir Douglas Haig, who had become Commander-in-Chief of the British forces in December 1915. A keen horseman, he believed cavalry still had an important part to play in the war. Few officers dared to disagree. Haig was a strong-willed and ambitious man who believed God was on his side. Even so, he expected heavy casualties at the Somme. But he thought it was a price worth paying for victory.

The blast of a massive underground mine, containing 20,400kg (45,000 pounds) of high explosive, detonated at 07:20, ten minutes before the first wave of British troops went over the top.

The walk-in

At 07:30 on July 1, the barrage lifted and whistles sounded along 40km (25 miles) of the Allied front – held by British troops to the north and a smaller French force to the south. The morning was hot and still, as thousands of soldiers obeyed the signal to step out into no-man's-land. They had been ordered to advance slowly, because their generals didn't trust them not to panic or stumble during the attack. So, they set off at a walk, expecting their opponents to be lying dead in their ruined trenches.

But the barrage had failed. Safe in their dugouts, the Germans heard the silence and guessed an attack was coming. They carried their machine guns to the surface and checked the barbed wire. It was still intact along much of the line.

Open Fire!

Thousands of soldiers died that morning, cut down by heavy machine-gun fire and shrapnel shells. The infantry broke on the German wire like a wave smashing into a cliff. Although some units made it through the wire and into the German trenches, they were soon dislodged by counterattacks. Only the French had some success, capturing a short section of the line in the south, where the German positions were weaker.

The cost

The Allies failed to make the breakthrough they had expected on the opening day of the battle. But, with the French still struggling at Verdun, they had to keep fighting at the Somme, in an attempt to wear out their opponents. The battle lasted until November, when rain flooded the battlefield. The Allies gained a few miles – but at a great cost.

More than a million men were killed or wounded in the Battle of the Somme. The Germans suffered the worst, with as many as 680,000 casualties. Around 125,000 men from Britain and its empire were killed, some 20,000 of them on the first day. Whole communities of young men – many from the Pals Battalions – simply vanished into the mud of no-man's-land, sending shock waves of loss and anger rippling through their hometowns.

> ### INTERNET LINK
>
> For a link to a website with photographs, art, movie footage and personal accounts of the Battle of the Somme, go to **www.usborne-quicklinks.com**

British infantry advance into no-man's-land through the tangled mess of barbed wire. This photograph comes from *The Battle of the Somme*, a movie made in 1916, which combined real footage of the battle with re-enactment scenes.

TRIALS AND TRAUMA

The trenches were a man-made hell where soldiers lived in constant fear for their lives. Some men found the pressure unbearable and went insane or ran away. But military courts had no sympathy for anyone breaking army rules and the punishments they used were often as brutal as the war itself.

This dejected young British soldier, suffering from shell shock, has been taken prisoner by the Germans. He is wearing waders that were given to many men to keep them dry in flooded trenches.

A bad case of nerves

There were few things more terrifying than sitting through days of heavy shelling. The ground shook like an earthquake and the incessant roar of explosions made it impossible to rest. Around one in fifty British trench soldiers suffered from a complete physical and mental collapse, known as shell shock, at some point in the fighting. At the time of the war, doctors didn't know much about stress, depression or mental breakdown. They thought shell shock was caused by the air pressure from exploding bombs disturbing a soldier's brain.

Some shell shock victims trembled with convulsions and couldn't talk or think clearly. Others cowered at the slightest noise. Rest was the only cure, and thousands of men were sent home to specialist hospitals. The less fortunate were granted a few weeks leave, then ordered back to the Front. If the prospect of more shelling was too much to bear their only hope of escape was suicide, self-wounding or desertion.

Tickets home

There were thousands of cases of self-wounding during the war, as soldiers shot themselves in the foot or hacked off a thumb. If the wound was serious enough, a man could be sent home for good. But army doctors had strict orders to investigate all suspicious injuries and anyone caught could expect harsh treatment in a prison hospital swiftly followed by a military trial.

Shot at dawn

Desertion, or going AWOL (Absent Without Leave) is one of the most serious crimes in any army. After a military trial that was often over in minutes, a dazed soldier could be sentenced to death by firing squad. Dozens of other crimes could warrant the death penalty, including self-wounding, cowardice or falling asleep on sentry duty. According to official claims, the British shot 346 soldiers, the French 133 and the Germans 48, but the real figures are probably much higher.

Dreaded punishments

For drunkenness and other petty crimes, offenders were usually given extra work duties or a short period behind bars. But British soldiers who misbehaved in this way could suffer 'Field Punishment No. 1' – being strapped or shackled to a post for several hours. Soldiers hated this torture. It humiliated and terrified the victim, as he couldn't run for cover if a stray enemy shell came over.

Two American soldiers have been made to wear signs on their backs – denouncing them as a 'straggler' and a 'deserter' – to humiliate them in front of their comrades.

Brothers in arms

However dreadful they were, the threat of punishments only partly explains why so many men put up with the trenches. Most soldiers showed incredible resilience and determination to do their duty. They stayed because they believed in what they were doing – or because they didn't want to let down their friends.

These troops are being treated for their injuries immediately after an attack, before being sent on to a hospital behind the front lines. The glazed expression of the man to the left suggests that he may be shell shocked.

WOMEN IN UNIFORM

It was not only on the home front that women played a vital part in the war. From the start of the conflict, they volunteered their services in hospitals, nursing sick and wounded soldiers. Some got even closer to the action as ambulance drivers and stretcher bearers, providing immediate medical care on the front line. But as the war went on, women were called upon to join the uniformed ranks of the armed forces too. Most worked behind the front lines, but a few women actually fought on the battlefield.

This British poster was designed to urge women to join the Women's Royal Naval Service, known as the Wrens.

Nurses under fire

Most hospitals were safe behind the front lines, but even there they were subject to enemy attacks. Every day, nurses had to cope with the harrowing sight of dead and mauled bodies, and to give their traumatized patients comfort and reassurance, as well as medical treatment. Closer to the fighting, many women showed amazing courage, risking their lives to drive ambulances and give First Aid, often under enemy fire.

A nurse cares for a severely wounded Belgian soldier in a hospital in Antwerp, 1915.

One of the most famous nurses of the First World War was a British woman named Edith Cavell. She worked in a Red Cross hospital in German-occupied Brussels. Although she treated refugees and soldiers of all nationalities, she also secretly helped hundreds of Allied soldiers in her care to escape from behind enemy lines. When the Germans discovered what she had been doing, they arrested her and executed her by firing squad.

These four mechanics of the Women's Royal Air Force are working on the fuselage of a fighter plane.

Supporting roles

All armed forces rely on the support of large numbers of non-combat staff, known as auxiliaries. They include cooks, clerks, engineers, telephone operators and dispatch riders. By 1917, many of the men performing these tasks were needed to make up the numbers on the front lines, so women were encouraged to take their places.

Warrior women

Most countries tried to protect their women from the dangers of battle, but the small Serbian army suffered such heavy losses that it had to take on female soldiers. One of them was a British woman named Flora Sandes. She had gone to Serbia as a nurse, but took up arms when the country was invaded. In Russia and Germany, a few women were so eager to fight, they pretended to be men.

INTERNET LINK

For links to websites where you can read extracts from nurses' own accounts of working on the front line, and find out more about the experiences of women in the armed forces during the First World War, go to www.usborne-quicklinks.com

Russian amazons

By mid-1917, the Russian army was in crisis, as thousands of men had deserted the ranks. A woman named Maria Bochkareva persuaded the government to let her set up a women's unit – the so-called 'Battalion of Death' – partly to shame the men into fighting again. The 2,000 strong battalion was involved in heavy fighting, and within just three months, there were only 250 left.

Shaven-headed women soldiers of the Russian 'Battalion of Death' stand to attention in their uniforms, 1917.

SHOCK TACTICS

With the Germans concentrating all their efforts on the Western Front, the maverick Russian general, Alexei Brusilov, launched a major assault against Austria-Hungary. The Brusilov Offensive, as it became known, was arguably Russia's most successful operation in the entire war. Much of Brusilov's success was down to his development of a radical new style of fighting: shock tactics.

A punishing attack

Allied commanders had planned to launch a summer offensive along the whole of the Eastern Front, at the same time as their push at the Somme. The Russians would attack the Germans to the north and the Austro-Hungarians to the south. But the Austro-Hungarian commander, General Conrad, had other plans. On May 15, he launched what he called a 'punishment expedition' in northern Italy. Conrad's troops soon broke through the Italian front line, and the Italians appealed to Russia for help.

Brusilov's plan

General Brusilov was in charge of Russian operations along the southern section of the Eastern Front, on the Austro-Hungarian frontier. In order to divert Conrad's troops away from Italy, he brought forward his part of the summer offensive. He also hoped he might be able to take back territory the Russians had lost in Galicia the year before.

Brusilov believed the best tactic was to take the enemy by surprise. He planned to attack on a wide front, digging tunnels, or saps, as close as possible to the Austro-Hungarian trenches without being detected. Then, specialized units of soldiers – 'shock troops' – would stage lightning attacks, blowing open holes in the Austro-Hungarian front line for the rest of the Russian army to advance through.

General Brusilov studies a map during the offensive that was named after him.

A surprising success

The attack began as dawn broke, on June 4. The Austro-Hungarians were taken completely by surprise, just as Brusilov had planned. His troops broke through enemy lines with ease, taking thousands of prisoners, as their opponents were stunned into surrender. To fight off the Russians, Conrad was forced to shut down operations on the Italian Front.

In July, Russian forces on the northern part of the Eastern Front also went on the offensive. But they were soon stopped in their tracks by fresh German troops, sent to reinforce their allies. In the south, Brusilov battled on successfully until September. By then, his troops had recaptured a belt of territory almost 100km (60 miles) wide. Around 600,000 Austro-Hungarians were killed or wounded.

This map shows the front line on the southern part of the Eastern Front during 1916.

Russian shock troops advance during the Brusilov Offensive, summer 1916. The Russians had spent the winter training new recruits and building up stocks of munitions. But, strengthening their army led to great hardship among the people back home.

Rumania's short war

The neutral Rumanian government watched all this with keen interest. Believing the Austro-Hungarians were all but defeated, they decided to throw in their lot with the Allies. Their main motive was to win Transylvania, an Austro-Hungarian province that was home to around three million ethnic Rumanians. On August 27, Rumanian troops invaded Austria-Hungary, through the Transylvanian Alps. It was an unwise move. German, Austro-Hungarian and Bulgarian troops soon forced them to retreat. On December 6, the Central Powers captured the Rumanian capital, Bucharest.

Passing glory

By mid-September, Brusilov's forces had advanced as far as the Carpathians. But they ground to a halt when they got beyond the reach of supplies or reserve troops. They were sent south to help the Rumanians in their failing campaign. By the end of the year, all the territory Brusilov had won was back in enemy hands. Russian troops had succeeded in bringing the Austro-Hungarian force to its knees, but they ended the year exhausted and demoralized.

SECRETS AND SPIES

Knowledge is power. Knowing what your enemy plans to do next, while keeping your own intentions secret, can mean the difference between victory and defeat. Throughout the war, both sides used spies to keep watch on each other, and took careful measures to prevent valuable information from falling into the wrong hands.

A Belgian firing squad takes aim during the execution of a captured German agent, October 1914.

Staking out the opposition

Even before the war, British agents in Germany had been busy collecting information. Their main focus was shipbuilding and arms supplies in the naval bases, but they also gathered road maps and train timetables – any 'intelligence' that might be useful in a military campaign. Meanwhile, German spies were doing the same thing in Britain. What neither country realized was that many of their agents were themselves under surveillance, from the very people they were spying on. As soon as war was declared, all suspected spies in enemy territory were swiftly rounded up and imprisoned.

INTERNET LINK

For links to websites where you can find out more about First World War espionage, and find out how to make invisible ink go to www.usborne-quicklinks.com

Homeland security

In Germany, all foreigners – merchant seamen and even a few tourists – were taken prisoner. In Britain, all Germans and Austro-Hungarians, including many who had lived there most of their lives, were classed as 'enemy aliens' and sent to internment camps for the rest of the war. With anti-German feeling running high, the British royal family changed their name, from the German-sounding Saxe-Coburg, to Windsor.

Governments brought in new laws limiting ownership of anything that might be used to contact the enemy. This included telephones, telegraph equipment, flagpoles and even pigeons. People were told to report anything suspicious. In the so-called 'spy mania' that followed, police investigated thousands of suspected spies, but very few turned out to be real.

Censors and code breakers

Throughout the war, governments on both sides, censored newspaper reports of the conflict. This helped to keep public opinion on their side, and prevented information from being published that might be of use to the other side. Postal services were censored too. Secret service officers opened and read all suspicious letters, intercepting messages to and from enemy agents, leading to the arrest of several spies.

In the trenches and out at sea, military orders had to be passed on by telephone or telegram. Spies could easily tap into lines or pick up wireless transmissions, so messages were usually sent in code. Unfortunately for the Germans, the Allies got hold of three of their naval codebooks, early in the war. From then on, British code breakers, based in Room 40 of the Admiralty headquarters, were able to intercept and decode most German naval signals. This gave them a huge advantage, particularly during the Battle of Jutland.

Spy tactics

Spies developed some ingenious ways of smuggling messages out of enemy territory. These included writing in invisible ink and concealing notes in hollowed-out coat buttons and glass eyes. Despite these tricks, many of the people involved in wartime espionage were untrained civilians, and they often got caught.

"If you could only send me some money, I could get my brother, who is in the navy, to give me all the navy movements..." This message, from a German spy in Britain, was written on sheet music in invisible ink. It was intercepted in the post by British intelligence.

Femme fatale

The most infamous spy of the war was a Dutch woman named Margareta Zelle. Part Javanese, she reinvented herself as an oriental princess and exotic dancer under the stage name of Mata Hari. During the war, her act was a huge hit with soldiers on leave, and she had a string of love affairs with military officers.

German agents paid her to gather information. But later she offered to work as a spy for the French too. This made her a double agent. When the Germans captured a French agent, Mata Hari was held to blame. She was arrested in Paris and shot at dawn on October 13, 1917.

Mata Hari, in full costume, performs the dance that made her the darling of the troops.

DESERT WARS

At the start of the war, the British had brought troops to the Middle East to defend their oil supplies. But they soon made plans to push further into Turkish territories. After Gallipoli, British commanders decided that the only way to topple the Turks was to provoke their Arab subjects to revolt.

A romantic hero: Thomas Edward Lawrence in traditional Arab dress

Stirring a revolt

Under the Young Turks, Arabs were treated as second-class citizens, and many had begun to talk of throwing off Turkish rule. In October 1914, the British High Commissioner in Egypt began negotiating with the Arab leader, Sherif Hussein of Mecca. He offered to supply money and arms for a revolt against the Turks, and promised that the Arabs would be left to rule their own lands after the war. In Cairo, the British set up the Arab Bureau, whose staff liaised with Arab leaders to build support for the revolt. Among them was an idealistic young intelligence officer named T.E. Lawrence – who later became famous as Lawrence of Arabia.

Meanwhile, British and Indian forces were advancing up the Tigris river into Mesopotamia. They had already captured Basra, Kurna and Kut, and in May 1915, they began to push north, toward Baghdad, the regional capital.

British under siege

In November 1915, British and Indian troops were close to Baghdad when they met tough Turkish resistance. Half their 8,500 men were killed or wounded and they retreated to Kut. But the Turks surrounded the city and held it under siege.

British forces tried to sail up the Tigris to rescue their beleaguered comrades, but heavy floods blocked their way. In March 1916, Lawrence undertook a secret mission, to attempt to pay the Turkish generals to end the siege. But they weren't interested. After 147 days under siege, with men dying like flies from sickness and starvation, the British finally surrendered on April 29.

Lawrence of Arabia

Before the war, Lawrence had learned Arabic and grown familiar with local customs, while studying archaeology in the Middle East. At the Arab Bureau, he gathered information about the Turks' military strategies, their strengths and weaknesses. With help from Lawrence and the Arab Bureau, Sherif Hussein finally took up arms against the Turks in June 1916. Within three months, Arab forces had captured Mecca, Jedda and Taif, and were advancing north.

Guerrilla tactics

In October, Lawrence joined Hussein's son Emir Feisal, in charge of part of the Arab army. He decided to adopt Arab dress. This irritated his British commanders, but it helped him to gain acceptance among his fellow fighters. It was practical too, as the head-cloth gave protection against the searing sun, wind and sand.

The Turkish army far outnumbered Arab forces, so Lawrence advised Feisal to use guerrilla tactics against them. They carried out night raids on Turkish camps, and mined bridges and train lines to sabotage their communications and supplies. This forced the Turks to divert large numbers of troops away from the fighting elsewhere, including Mesopotamia.

A change of fortunes

The British saw their chance to renew their campaign in Mesopotamia. So they sent in reinforcements, heavy artillery and a new commander, Sir Stanley Maude. He made rapid progress, retaking Kut in February 1917, and capturing Baghdad on March 11. With much of Mesopotamia now in Allied hands and the Arabs in revolt, the Turks looked close to defeat.

British troops march triumphantly into Baghdad, past a large crowd of local onlookers.

INTERNET LINK

For a link to a website where you can find out more about Lawrence of Arabia and the Arabs' guerrilla tactics, go to **www.usborne-quicklinks.com**

This photograph, taken by Lawrence from the back of a camel, shows Emir Feisal (second from the right, dressed in white) leading his guerrilla forces through the desert.

Two anti-tsarist Russian soldiers ride through Petrograd on the running board of a motor car, March 1917. One of them has attached a red flag to his bayonet.

CRISIS AND RESOLUTION

By 1917, three years of fighting had taken their toll on soldiers and civilians on both sides, and many began to demand an end to the conflict. In Russia, the people overthrew the government and pulled out of the war. But, while Russia was in turmoil, the Allies gained a strong new member, as the US finally joined the war. By spring of 1918, both Allied and German commanders were determined to bring the war to a climax, by launching one last big push on the Western Front. Eventually, the Central Powers were forced to admit defeat. The war finally ended on November 11, 1918.

RIOTS AND REBELS

After several years of war, soldiers and civilians were pushed to the limits of their endurance. Facing food shortages at home and slaughter on the battlefields, some people took to the streets to demand change. Their protests sparked riots, mutinies – even revolution.

Trouble in Dublin

Ireland was part of the United Kingdom, but Irish nationalists wanted more control over their own affairs. In 1914, the British government had agreed that Ireland could set up their own parliament, but the deal was postponed by the outbreak of war. The nationalists agreed to wait, and thousands of them enlisted to fight for the British army.

But a rebel group called the Irish Republican Brotherhood saw the war as the perfect opportunity to claim total independence. On April 24, 1916, just over a thousand rebels took control of central Dublin, in what became known as the Easter Rising. After five days of bloody street battles with British soldiers, the republicans surrendered. Ireland remained in turmoil, and the soldiers who'd gone to fight for Britain would return after the war to a divided and unsettled land.

French troops resting, by Christopher Nevinson. The French soldiers in this painting have stopped by the roadside on their way to the front. They look tired and despondent, as though all fighting spirit has left them.

Breaking ranks

By the start of 1917, the French army was exhausted and demoralized. Soldiers complained that the government didn't understand the miseries of the trenches. They wanted better food, more leave and an end to the large-scale offensives that cost thousands of lives. Some infantrymen started to 'baa' and bleat whenever they saw an officer – like lambs being led to the slaughterhouse.

In April 1917, the French commander, Robert Nivelle, launched a massive assault on the Western Front. He promised a quick breakthrough and an end to the war, but his offensive failed and the resulting casualties were shocking. Feeling betrayed, around half of the French army mutinied against their commanders by refusing to attack. The mutiny lasted for three months. Remarkably, the Germans failed to take advantage of the situation because they had no idea what was going on. In August, the French brought in a new commander, Philippe Pétain. He ended the crisis by offering better conditions for his men, helping to raise their morale.

In central Dublin during the Easter Rising, British troops take cover behind a makeshift street barricade made from pieces of furniture.

INTERNET LINK

For a link to a website with photographs, articles, posters and rebel songs from the Easter Rising, or to explore the luxurious lifestyle of the Russian royal family through an online scrapbook, go to **www.usborne-quicklinks.com**

Give us bread

Long before the war, many Russians had been unhappy with the tsars, who had the power to rule the country as they pleased. In 1905, factory workers in the capital city, St. Petersburg, protested against Tsar Nicholas II. This sparked strikes and riots in other towns, and he was forced to set up a parliament to rule with him. But he made sure it had very little power, and most Russians still had no say in the way their country was run.

The war caused terrible food shortages. Many Russians, who were already living in dire poverty, began to starve. People blamed the Tsar for their suffering and for the carnage at the front. They took to the streets, demanding more food, democratic elections and an end to the war. In March 1917, riots broke out in St. Petersburg – which had been renamed Petrograd at the start of the war, to sound less German. The Tsar ordered the soldiers of the city garrison to crush them, but they mutinied and joined the rioters instead. The Tsar abdicated on March 15, and new government took charge. But the riots were only the beginning of a greater revolution that would explode across Russia later that year.

Rough treatment

The most serious British mutiny was at a tough training camp in France. When a soldier was unfairly arrested at the camp in September 1917, thousands of troops turned on the military police and chased them into town. Two days of rioting followed, until soldiers armed with wooden clubs put an end to the protest. To prevent news of the unrest reaching the enemy, the whole incident was declared top secret and covered up by the British government.

A mutinous Russian army officer distributes anti-tsarist newspapers to an eager mob in a Moscow street, February 1917.

PEACE, BREAD AND LAND

Tsar Nicholas' downfall came when he lost the loyalty of his army. But, instead of learning from the Tsar's failure, the new government was determined to keep fighting the war. This unpopular decision brought anger and resentment, still felt by many soldiers and civilians, back to the surface. Recent history was about to repeat itself.

A losing battle

In June 1917, the head of the government, Alexander Kerensky, appointed General Brusilov to lead a new offensive against Austria-Hungary. Brusilov launched the attack on June 18, sending shock troops ahead of regular forces. Things began well for Brusilov until German troops launched a strong counterattack. Within three weeks, the Russian army was in retreat and in total disarray, as even its commanding officers turned against the government.

Similar to the British poster of Kitchener, this Russian revolutionary poster urges peasants to join a workers' cooperative.

INTERNET LINK

For a link to a website with pictures and more information on the Russian Revolution, Lenin and the Bolshevik leaders, go to **www.usborne-quicklinks.com**

Storming the Winter Palace. This re-enactment was staged in 1921, to celebrate the anniversary of the 1917 revolution.

Power to the people

While the Russian army was suffering at the hands of German forces, at home the government came under attack from a political party called the Bolsheviks. They urged people to overthrow the government and take control for themselves. They called on peasant farmers to seize the land from their landlords, industrial workers to take control of the factories and soldiers to abandon their posts.

Storming the palace

On October 24, 1917, Bolshevik troops surrounded the Winter Palace in Petrograd, the seat of the new government. The building was defended by a small number of soldiers who remained loyal to Kerensky. But they put up little resistance as the revolutionaries stormed the palace, arrested Kerensky's government and seized power. Two days later, the Bolsheviks declared their leader, Lenin, head of the new government.

End of the line

Meanwhile, Tsar Nicholas and his family were taken prisoner and hidden in the remote Siberian city of Yekaterinburg. When their captors heard reports that anti-Bolshevik troops were approaching the area, they worried that they might be attacked and the Tsar set free. So the Boshevik guards lined up their royal prisoners and shot them dead.

In October 1917, Lenin delivers a rousing revolutionary speech to a crowd of soldiers and workers.

Lenin's promise

The Bolshevik Revolution had been quick and fairly bloodless, but that didn't mean that everyone in Russia supported the new regime. To unite the people behind him, Lenin promised "peace, bread and land" for all, and called on European nations to end the war. He didn't expect the Allies or the Central Powers to agree to a cease-fire, but he hoped that their refusal might help to provoke revolution in other countries. To his dismay, the Germans offered to make peace, on the condition that they could take control of much of European Russia. When the Bosheviks refused, German troops attacked, forcing them back to the negotiating table.

From war to civil war

On March 3, 1918, Lenin's foreign minister, Leon Trotsky, finally signed the peace treaty between Russia and the Central Powers at the Polish city of Brest-Litovsk. The treaty forced the Bolsheviks to hand over much of western Russia to the Germans, costing the country a third of its population, half its industries and almost all of its coal reserves. Many Russian patriots were furious at what they saw as a shameful peace. With Allied support, anti-Bolsheviks took up arms against the Bolsheviks. Russia's part in the First World War was over, but the country was now plunged into a civil war that would last for nearly three years.

Tsar Nicholas II poses in the snow with his children and nephews, around the time of his abdication in March 1917.

WAKING THE GIANT

In the face of Allied and American outrage after the sinking of the *Lusitania*, the Germans had scaled down their U-boat attacks. But from February 1917, they began torpedoing all ships bound for Allied ports without warning. This was the turning point for the American president, Woodrow Wilson, who had struggled for years to keep his country out of the war.

U-boat aggression

German navy commanders promised the Kaiser that their U-boats could starve Britain into submission within five months. But the ruthless sinking of merchant and passenger ships infuriated Wilson, who believed the oceans should be the "free highways" of the world. After the sinking of the *Lusitania*, he had warned the Germans that America wouldn't tolerate any further loss of life at sea.

On February 26, a journalist named Floyd Gibbons reported a torpedo attack on a British passenger ship, *Laconia*, off the west coast of Ireland. Gibbons had survived the sinking, but three Americans died in the icy Atlantic waters. When his article was published, it provoked a debate across the USA – how much longer could the country keep out of the war?

Diplomatic skulduggery

Wilson had other reasons to be furious about Germany's actions. In January 1917, the German foreign secretary, Arthur Zimmermann, had sent a coded telegram to his ambassador in Mexico. Zimmermann ordered the ambassador to make a secret pact with the Mexican and Japanese governments, in case America entered the war. Germany promised the Mexicans "generous financial support" and control of Texas, New Mexico and Arizona if they would join the Central Powers.

Zimmermann's telegram ranks as one of the most explosive documents in history. It was intercepted by British code breakers at Room 40, who presented US officials with a copy in February. The following month, the story broke in newspapers around the world.

The British and American flags are flown from the top of a British tank as it is paraded past the Flatiron building in New York, April, 1917.

A change of heart

The President was a peace-loving man, who had used the campaign slogan "he kept us out of the war" to win the 1916 election. But the U-boat threat to American ships and civilians, combined with Germany's shadowy approaches to Mexico, were too much for him. In early April, he asked the US Congress to declare war. On April 6, Wilson announced to the world that the United States was at war with the Central Powers.

This painting, by Edmund Tarbell, depicts President Woodrow Wilson in a scholarly pose at his desk.

Peacemaker

Wilson was anxious to persuade his critics that his intention in joining the war was "to make the world safe for democracy" – not to make territorial gains. He put together a secret panel of scholars and soldiers – known as 'The Inquiry' – to report on the European situation. Using their findings, Wilson started drafting a plan for a League of Nations, which would promote lasting peace, democracy and free international trade. In January 1918, Wilson set out this ambitious vision in a speech that became known as the Fourteen Points.

Countdown

Wilson's aim might have been world peace but first he had to help smash the Central Powers. At the beginning of 1917, the US army was only 100,000 strong, but after a huge recruitment drive, and the introduction of conscription (the draft), it would land over two million men in Europe

This recruitment poster copies the famous Kitchener poster of 1914.

before the end of the war. Fleets shipping troops across the Atlantic were protected by naval convoys so Germany's U-boats were powerless to stop them.

While America geared itself up for a massive military expedition, Allied leaders celebrated the promise of a fresh army fighting on their side. In November, the British prime minister, Lloyd George suggested the formation of a new Supreme War Council, with a seat for each Allied nation – including the United States. Help was on its way.

INTERNET LINK

For links to websites where you can read the Zimmerman telegram and find out more about President Wilson, go to www.usborne-quicklinks.com

American commander John Pershing (far left) inspects a battalion of African-American troops. Around 200,000 black Americans served in the war, but they were segregated from their white comrades, and few saw active combat.

DROWNING IN MUD

While they waited for the US troops to come to their aid, British generals came up with a plan to break the U-boat stranglehold by capturing German ports along the Belgian coast. It resulted in a disastrous battle that was one of the most heartbreaking of the war.

Third time lucky

The British commander, Sir Douglas Haig, believed the German army was exhausted after the Battle of the Somme. So he calculated that a quick strike through Flanders would break their line, opening the way for his cavalry troops to occupy the U-boat ports of Ostend and Zeebrugge.

Haig's faith in his plan wasn't shared by the British prime minister, David Lloyd George. He argued that it would be wiser to wait for the US army to arrive. But Haig insisted it was vital to keep up the pressure on the Western Front. So, on July 31, Allied troops launched the infamous Third Battle of Ypres, which has become known as Passchendaele.

Stuck in the mud at Passchendaele, two horses are struggling to drag a water cart out of the quagmire and back onto the wooden track.

No place for fighting

The Passchendaele Ridge, near Ypres was a stretch of high ground held by the Germans, surrounded by low, open plains. It was well defended: fresh battalions waited miles behind the line and hundreds of bombproof machine gun nests and artillery posts overlooked no-man's-land. They even had stores of mustard gas ready to release.

Haig decided to shell the ridge for ten solid days before sending his men over the top. But the area around it was a marsh, already churned up by years of shelling. Haig's barrage turned it into a muddy slime. Then it started to rain.

INTERNET LINK

For links to websites where you can see photographs and read eyewitness accounts of Passchendaele, go to
www.usborne-quicklinks.com

Mud warriors

Weather experts had warned Haig about the high rainfall in Flanders, but the rain in the summer of 1917 was the worst for 30 years. Shell craters in no-man's-land filled with water and the only way to make progress across the quagmire was to creep over duckboards – wooden slats, tied together. Wounded or exhausted men often slipped into the mud and disappeared. Tens of thousands of them still lie buried there today.

The creeping barrage

But Haig pressed on with the battle, ordering his soldiers to attack under the protection of a new artillery tactic, known as a creeping barrage. This relied on gunners to shell the ground immediately ahead of charging infantry. As the men advanced, the gunners adjusted their range to keep shells landing just before them. If all went to plan, the infantry would be supported up to their target – which they would hold until reinforcements arrived. But, in the chaos of battle, creeping barrages were notoriously difficult to control.

Australian soldiers walk across a duckboard track over the blasted Passchendaele battlefield, in this picture taken by the Australian photographer, Frank Hurley.

Young lions

By October, courageous British and Australian troops had made some inroads into the enemy line using the creeping barrage tactic. But the suffering of the men – and the thousands of horse teams used to pull artillery pieces – was appalling. With no hope of a breakthrough, Haig still resisted calls to stop the fighting. It was a decision that baffled even his closest supporters.

There is a famous remark made by two German generals. Some historians have used it to argue that the lives of British soldiers were squandered by their commanders. One of them claimed that the British fought like lions. "True," the other replied, "but they are lions led by donkeys." Haig always stubbornly refused to allow heavy casualty figures to change his objectives. He triumphed in the end, but the infantry paid a terrible price.

On November 6, Canadian soldiers finally captured the village of Passchendaele and Haig agreed to end the battle. But the U-boat bases had escaped attack. Only five months later, the Germans would retake every inch of the ground they had lost.

"I died in hell - (They called it Passchendaele)."

War poet, Siegfried Sassoon

BACKS TO THE WALL

With Russia out of the war, the Germans had a million combat-ready soldiers to move to the Western Front. Before the US troops could arrive in strength, the German commanders decided to launch what they called their Spring Offensive. This meant throwing everything they had into a series of desperate battles.

Lightning strikes

The Germans had spent the latter part of 1917 planning the offensive and training their men in new fighting skills. Just before dawn on March 21, they began shelling the Allied lines with a "devil's orchestra" of roaring guns, as one soldier described it. The barrage lasted for five hours. Before the defenders could recover, groups of German infantry started appearing out of the morning fog.

These were storm troopers, elite soldiers armed with light machine guns, flamethrowers and grenades. They looked for weak points in defensive positions and forced their way deep into the Allies' trench system, always advancing. Allied soldiers soon found themselves cut off from each other and outflanked by waves of regular German troops following the first assault force.

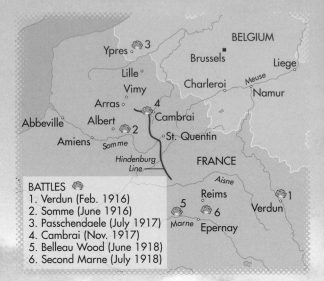

This map of the Western Front shows the sites of the main battles of the second half of the war and the Hindenburg Line – a vast network of trenches and concrete dug-outs.

BATTLES
1. Verdun (Feb. 1916)
2. Somme (June 1916)
3. Passchendaele (July 1917)
4. Cambrai (Nov. 1917)
5. Belleau Wood (June 1918)
6. Second Marne (July 1918)

> **INTERNET LINK**
> For a link to a website where you can view an animated map of the German Spring Offensive of 1918, go to www.usborne-quicklinks.com

A new commander

The Allied line buckled along an 80km (50 miles) front, forcing them to retreat. As the Germans pushed closer to Paris and threatened the Channel ports, Allied politicians decided the troops needed decisive leadership to deal with the crisis. So, they appointed a French general, Ferdinand Foch, as overall commander to coordinate the actions of all the Allied forces on the Western Front.

To the last man

By April, the British were fighting for their lives against ferocious German attacks. Sir Douglas Haig sent his soldiers what became known as his 'Backs to the Wall' order: "Every position must be held to the last man…With our backs to the wall, and believing in the justice of our cause, each one of us must fight on to the end." Haig was asking his men for one last, heroic effort – and it worked. The British fought with all the skill and toughness they had gained in three years of trench fighting.

Under General Foch's overall command, French, American, British and Italian troops fought to victory at the Second Battle of the Marne in July. The Spring Offensive faltered, and the Germans went into retreat. They had captured land, enemy guns and thousands of prisoners, but they had advanced too quickly. They had no artillery support, and few supplies.

Running on empty

Britain was getting through the U-boat blockade by organizing their merchant ships into convoys protected by destroyer escorts. But the Royal Navy's blockade against Germany was stronger than ever. There were food shortages in German cities and the army didn't have enough meat or fresh produce to feed their men. German troops were so hungry they stopped their attacks to loot Allied dugouts and food tents, gorging themselves on fresh bread, eggs and wine.

Dark days

On August 8, the Allies broke through the German line at Amiens, prompting General Ludendorff to describe it as a "black day" for his army. By September his troops were retreating to the Hindenburg Line – the defensive position they had held the year before. Exhausted and malnourished, thousands of them fell prey to a deadly flu virus. It could kill a man overnight, and would sweep around the world later that year. But disease was only one of the dangers they faced. The Allies were preparing another massive attack of their own.

Past the body of a French soldier, German troops advance through smoke and fire during the Spring Offensive.

DEATH THROES

The failure of the Spring Offensive broke the fighting spirit of the German army. Most soldiers were tired of the war. Their families were starving and men who had been home returned to the front with stories of strikes and mutinies. Allied troops drew closer, but the Kaiser refused to surrender.

American 'doughboys' in action during the Battle of Belleau Wood, June 1918

Ready and willing

The arrival of the American Expeditionary Force, commanded by General 'Black Jack' Pershing, dealt a crushing blow to German morale. The fresh-faced American soldiers landing in France were nicknamed 'doughboys' by the local people, probably because they looked so plump and healthy. Most of them had no battle experience, but they fought like tigers. Any doubts about the quality and bravery of these new troops were settled in June 1918, at the Battle of Belleau Wood.

Floyd Gibbons – the reporter who had survived a run-in with a U-boat – was once again in the thick of it. He was following US Marines in a charge across open fields when they were caught in heavy machine-gun fire. Gibbons was hit three times and lost an eye as he tried to save an injured soldier. More than 5,700 Marines were wounded or killed in the battle.

Allied power

It wasn't just the arrival of the doughboys that depressed German soldiers. The Allies had a constant supply of food, guns and ammunition, whereas German shops and factories were running out of goods. Allied planes ruled the skies and their ships prowled the seas. On land, they enjoyed yet another advantage, which had proved a formidable weapon in November 1917, at the Battle of Cambrai: the tank.

Ironsides

Apart from a few experimental prototypes and captured vehicles, the Germans had no tanks of their own. They trained their gunners to target them on the battlefield, but they could never stop them all. Tanks carried machine guns and light artillery pieces. They climbed hills, forded streams and cleared paths through wire for attacking infantry. The Allies were preparing for an assault on the Hindenburg Line, and tanks would play a vital role.

Closing in

On September 12, an all-American force stormed and captured German trenches close to Verdun. The Allied war machine was at last in a position to strike at the Hindenburg Line. On September 26, a combined force of French, British and American armies attacked. They used heavy artillery to break up the wire and concrete fortifications, and sent tanks equipped with metal cribs or bundles of roped logs, known as fascines, to fill any deep ditches.

After four days of savage battle, the heart of the Hindenburg Line was torn open. British troops and soldiers from the British colonies advanced through. Overwhelmed, the Germans began to retreat, fighting their pursuers every step of the way.

Kaiser Wilhelm studies battle plans with his two military commanders, Field Marshal Hindenburg (left) and General Ludendorff (right).

Biting the bullet

Germany's proud military commanders, Hindenburg and Ludendorff, finally accepted that the war was lost. With rebellious soldiers and civilians marching in the streets demanding a new government, even the Kaiser agreed that it was time to negotiate for peace with the Allies, without the disgrace of having to surrender. In October, he sent officials to propose a cease-fire, or armistice.

But, even with his empire crumbling around him, the Kaiser still thought Germany could end the war without losing too much power or territory. He wouldn't listen to any suggestions that he might be forced to give up his position as supreme ruler. But he was unaware of the disaster that was overtaking his country. Germany was facing nothing less than total ruin.

British troops march alongside tanks as they lumber toward the Hindenburg Line, September 1918. On top of the tanks are 'cribs' – cages to be dropped into trenches, enabling tanks to roll over the top.

ARMAGEDDON

While the Germans were losing control of the Western Front, the Turks came under pressure in the Middle East. The Arabs continued their guerrilla war in Hejaz, and the British decided to invade Palestine and Syria. If they succeeded, they hoped this would be enough to knock the Turks out of the war for good.

Waving the white flag. The mayor of Jerusalem (with a stick) surrenders to two British sergeants.

Pushing into Palestine

In July 1917, the Arabs scored one of their most important victories by capturing the Red Sea port of Akaba. Throughout 1916, British forces, made up of Australian cavalry and camel-mounted troops, and Indian infantry, had advanced from Egypt to occupy Sinai. Now they could use Akaba as a supply depot for an invasion of Palestine.

The British brought in a vigorous new commander, Edmund Allenby, to put their plan into action. He was under strict instruction to take the Palestinian capital, Jerusalem, by Christmas. In October, he overwhelmed the Turkish garrison at Gaza with an artillery assault, and used a massive cavalry charge to beat them into a retreat. On December 9, 1917, Allenby marched into Jerusalem. The holy city fell to the Allies two weeks ahead of schedule.

Double deals

From the outset of war in the Middle East, the British government had promised Arab leaders that they could rule their own lands independently after the war. But, unknown to the Arabs, they also made a secret pact with the French – the Sykes-Picot Agreement – to divide the region into areas that would be either French or British-run.

To muddy the waters still further, a powerful group of Jews from around the world, known as Zionists, had designs on Palestine too. They had long been campaigning to create a Jewish homeland there, where they could settle. As Allenby approached Jerusalem, the British foreign secretary, Arthur Balfour, wrote to Lord Rothschild, a leading Zionist, to declare his support. These dealings were at odds with the Arab cause, and when Lawrence found out, he was furious.

General Allenby makes his formal entry to Jerusalem. He marches behind the British governor of the city.

The road to Damascus

Lawrence and Feisal felt bitterly betrayed by the British government, but they continued to fight beside Allenby's troops. Blowing up the Hejaz train line, the Arabs prevented Turkish troops in Medina from moving north. This gave Allenby the edge he needed to launch the final big battle of his campaign. Fought near Megiddo (the site of the Biblical battle of Armageddon) in September 1918, it was a decisive victory for the Allies. Now, the road to Damascus, the Syrian capital, was wide open.

On October 1, the Arabs stormed Damascus and set up their own government, with Emir Feisal at the head. But, just two days later, Allenby caught up with them and announced that Syria would not be run by the Arabs, but by the French. Outraged, Lawrence immediately headed back to England to continue his campaign for Arab independence. Now his battles would be with Allied politicians.

Cavalry troops played a key role in the war in the Middle East. Here, Australian Light Horse regiments are advancing on Damascus. Sitting at the wayside are Turkish troops taken prisoner after the Battle of Megiddo.

A colossus falls

When the Russians pulled out of the war, Enver Pasha had sent troops to the Russian border, to regain territory the Turks had lost in the Caucasus. But this diverted their already depleted manpower away from Mesopotamia, where British troops advanced up the Tigris to take Mosul. When Allenby moved north through Syria, and seized Aleppo, the exhausted Turks finally gave in. On October 30, they signed an armistice and control over Turkish territory in the Middle East was split between the Allies. The colossal Ottoman empire – that had dominated the Middle East and the eastern Mediterranean for four centuries – had come to an end.

The Middle East in 1918

THE TIME FOR PEACE

With the German army retreating from France, and Turkey out of the war, the other Central Powers collapsed like a house of cards. They had staked everything on a brutal war of expansion. Defeat would cost them their empires.

A sinking ship

On September 15, 1918, an Allied force of French, Serbian, British, Greek and Italian troops, all based in Salonika, launched a daring assault against the rocky Bulgarian frontier. Thinking the war was lost, thousands of Bulgarian troops deserted. On September 28, their government signed a peace deal with the Allies.

Breaking strain

Many of the ethnic groups and member states that made up the Austro-Hungarian empire had long been demanding independence. The young emperor, Karl I, was desperate to save his fragile empire. In October 1918, he offered the member states more control over the way they were governed, but it was too little, too late. By the end of the month, Poland had claimed independence and Czech and Serb groups had broken away to form the new nations of Czechoslovakia and The Kingdom of Serbs, Croats and Slovenes – later renamed Yugoslavia. On November 1, Hungary, too, split from Austria.

The armistice between Germany and the Allies was signed in this train carriage. The negotiations were led by the Supreme Allied Commander, Ferdinand Foch (second on the right).

A final battle

As Karl's empire disintegrated, the Italians launched a furious attack against his army in the south of Austria. In the Battle of Vittorio Veneto they smashed their way into the country, capturing men and guns until the Austrians begged for peace on November 3. The emperor was forced to abandon his throne a few weeks later. The empire that had played a key role in starting the war, vanished forever from the map.

Army trucks parade the streets of London as they bring jubilant British soldiers home. It was several months before all the men were allowed to return from the front, causing resentment and frustration for many soldiers and their families.

Karl I succeeded his great uncle, Franz Josef I, to the Austro-Hungarian throne in the winter of 1916. Many of his people mistrusted him because his wife was Italian. He is pictured here, with his family, living in Switzerland after the war.

Sailors mutiny

On November 3, German sailors refused to take the High Seas Fleet into the North Sea. The time for heroic gestures was over. Germany's leaders were left with no allies, an unreliable army and a mutinous navy. There were riots in the streets and people were talking of another revolution, like the one in Russia. Generals and politicians bickered about who was to blame, while their soldiers were still being killed on the battlefields.

Disgrace and defeat

General Ludendorff was dismissed from his post and a new German government asked for peace. But the Allies had refused to discuss the terms of an armistice while the Kaiser was still in power. Wilhelm's generals told him the army could no longer be trusted to obey his orders. On November 9, Kaiser Wilhelm II abdicated and boarded a train for neutral Holland, where he would live out his days in permanent exile. This bitter and lonely old warhorse never forgave his officers for abandoning him.

At 11:00 on November 11, 1918 – the eleventh hour of the eleventh day of the eleventh month – church bells rang across Europe. The fighting was over and it was time for the men to come home.

PEACE AND ITS AFTERMATH

Even as people around the world celebrated the end of the war, they knew that life would never be the same again. The millions who had died could never be replaced. And governments argued about the best way to keep the peace. But perhaps the hardest adjustment was for soldiers who returned home, broken in body and spirit, unable to forget or make sense of the horrors of the war they had survived.

In October 1918, British soldiers are given a heroes' welcome as they march into Lille, a French city that was occupied by the Germans throughout the war.

COMING TO TERMS

The armistice of November 1918 brought the fighting to an end. In January 1919, the Allied leaders invited diplomats from 32 nations to meet in Paris, to thrash out the international agreements that would be needed to keep the peace. But many of them disagreed about the terms, and the leaders of the defeated nations weren't even consulted. It was never going to be possible to please everyone.

The Treaty of Versailles

The peace talks were led by the prime ministers of Britain and France, David Lloyd George and Georges Clemenceau, and US President Woodrow Wilson. All three wanted to stop Germany from starting another war, but they disagreed about the best way to do it. Clemenceau and Lloyd George wanted to punish the Germans, but Wilson was more interested in setting up agreements that would prevent future wars. In the end, the three leaders reached an uneasy compromise set out in the Treaty of Versailles – so-called because it was signed at the Palace of Versailles, outside Paris.

The League of Nations

One of the first things agreed at the conference was Wilson's plan to set up a League of Nations. This would be a diplomatic organization in which international disputes could be discussed and resolved peacefully. It had limited success, because its members disagreed on how it should be run, and, ironically, the US never joined. Eventually it was replaced, after the Second World War, by the United Nations.

Punishing Germany

To limit the Germans' power to start another war, the treaty forced them to make huge cuts in the size of their military forces, and to hand over their colonies overseas. They even had to give up territories in Europe too. These included Polish, French and Danish lands conquered during the 18th and 19th centuries, as well as parts of France, Belguim and Russia that the Germans had occupied during the war.

Germans take to the streets of Berlin to protest against losing the territories of Danzig and Posen after the Treaty of Versailles.

War guilt

Perhaps the most controversial part of the treaty was the 'war guilt' clause, which stated that Germany was to blame for starting the war. To compensate for the damage done during the fighting, the Allies ordered Germany to pay them huge sums of money. These payments – known as 'reparations' – were eventually set at £6,600,000,000 – a sum so big, the Germans estimated it would take until 1984 to pay it off.

Reactions in Germany

Although German politicians weren't invited to the Paris conference, they were summoned to Versailles to sign the treaty. They were shocked by how harsh the terms were, and at first they refused to sign. The German people bitterly resented the war guilt clause, as they felt they had only played a part in starting the war. Many staged street protests, but they had no choice but to accept it.

On June 28, 1919, the Germans reluctantly signed the Treaty of Versailles. Exactly five years after the assassination of Archduke Franz Ferdinand that had started it all, the First World War was officially over.

David Lloyd George (left), Georges Clemenceau (middle) and Woodrow Wilson – nicknamed the 'Big Three' – at the Paris peace conference in 1919.

REDRAWING THE MAP

With the Treaty of Versailles settled, further treaties were negotiated, to divide up lands held by Austria-Hungary, the Turkish empire and Bulgaria. Much of the map of the world was redrawn, as territories changed hands, national boundaries shifted and new countries were created. It wasn't a peaceful process, and has continued to cause unrest, and even armed conflict, in some of these regions ever since.

The day allotted for turning over territory to Rumania saw unrest in Hungary, as people tried, unsuccessfully, to resist the changes imposed on them.

New beginnings

When Austria-Hungary broke up, at the end of the war, the new countries of Czechoslovakia and Yugoslavia came into existence. Poland, which hadn't existed as an independent country since 1795, was put back on the map too.

To the north, Finland, Estonia, Latvia and Lithuania had been part of Russia until they were handed over to Germany under the Brest-Litovsk Treaty. The post-war treaties now recognized all these new countries as independent states, and set their official borders.

This map shows the new boundaries of Europe in 1924. Local disputes over territories meant that several revisions were made to the treaties of 1919.

Drawing the lines

As well as giving the new nations a chance to rule themselves, many of the changes in Europe were designed to reduce the power of the defeated nations. Austria, Hungary and Bulgaria were reduced to a fraction of their former size and deprived of many of their industrial resources, as much of their land was handed over to the surrounding countries. The Allied leaders hoped Czechoslovakia would provide a barrier between Austria and Germany, and that Yugoslavia would be big and powerful enough to bring peace and stability to the Balkans.

With the demands of so many countries to meet, the representatives of Britain, France, Italy and the USA often found it easier to make decisions without consulting the leaders of the smaller nations affected. This caused angry resentment in eastern Europe. People suddenly found themselves separated from their families by the new country borders and lumped together with people from different ethnic groups, whose language and culture they didn't share. So, right from the start, there were tensions, and sometimes violence.

Emir Feisal (front) and his Arab delegation, including Lawrence of Arabia (right of Feisal), at the Paris Peace Conference in 1919.

Broken promises

The former Turkish Ottoman empire was broken up too. The northern part was supposed to become the independent nation of Turkey, but Allied troops continued to occupy the region long after the treaties had been signed. Outraged, Turkish nationalists, led by General Mustafa Kemal, fought against the terms of the treaties. They drove out the occupying forces and eventually declared the independent Republic of Turkey in 1923.

During the war, the Allies had promised Arab leaders control of the Middle East. But they went back on their word, carving up most of the region into 'mandates' – states run by Britain and France, under the watch of the League of Nations. Half of Palestine was set aside as a homeland for Jewish people from around the world. But all this was met with armed resistance, so new treaties were brought in, during the 1920s, to give Arab leaders more control. The region has been troubled ever since.

This map shows the national boundaries in the Middle East in 1924. It also shows which mandates were run by France, and which were controlled by Britian.

INTERNET LINK

For links to websites where you can see maps and cartoons of the post-war treaties, and explore an interactive timeline of events in the Middle East since the war, go to www.usborne-quicklinks.com

THE GLORY AND THE PITY

While politicians argued in Paris, soldiers prepared themselves to return home from the front, uncertain how they would explain their experiences to their families. Some turned to poetry, written by soldiers in the trenches, to make sense of the suffering and destruction they had seen. Many of these poems are so powerful, that they are still widely read today.

Rupert Brooke's original notes of *The Soldier* written on army writing paper

Warrior poets

Poetry was taken very seriously at the time of the war, as people believed it was the best way to express powerful feelings and beliefs – including love of your country. As they explored what it meant to fight and die for their homeland, some writers looked back to Greek and Roman poets for inspiration. These ancient poets had often argued that death in battle was the ultimate heroism.

A soldier takes advantage of a quiet moment to do some writing.

England's finest

Rupert Brooke was a talented young poet fascinated by the idea of risking his life for his country. His poem *The Soldier* made him an instant literary star with its patriotic language:

If I should die, think only this of me:
That there's some corner of a foreign field
Which is for ever England. There shall be
In that rich earth a richer dust concealed;
A dust whom England bore...

Brooke's words seemed to capture a spirit of duty and willing self-sacrifice that gripped many soldiers at the opening of the war. He never fought, but he did die for his country. He enlisted and sailed for Gallipoli in March 1915. During the voyage he was bitten by a mosquito and died of blood poisoning. Brooke was buried on a Greek island, the home of the ancient warrior poets he so admired.

Broken hearts and minds

Men from across Europe and around the world went to war with visions of glory and heroism on the battlefield, but most were shocked by what they discovered in the trenches. Soldiers from every side expressed similar feelings of pain, loss and despair. Some even used their writing to demand an end to the conflict.

In 1917, a British poet and army officer, Siegfried Sassoon, wrote a letter to British newspapers describing the war as evil and unjust. Sassoon could have been shot, but the army decided he must be suffering from shell shock and sent him to a hospital in Scotland. Sassoon's poetry was well known by this time, and lots of his fellow patients asked him for help with their writing. Among them was a gentle young officer called Wilfred Owen, who would later become one of the most famous poets of the First World War.

INTERNET LINK

For a link to a website where you can read more poems by First World War poets, and find out more about their lives, go to
www.usborne-quicklinks.com

A doomed poet

Owen was a shy and quiet man whose nerves had been shattered by months of hard fighting. He hated the war, but returned to the trenches in 1918 because he felt it was his duty to describe what was happening there. Owen wasn't interested in patriotism. His poetry was concerned with the hearts and minds of common soldiers.

In *Dulce et Decorum Est*, Owen mocks the idea of proud warriors enjoying noble deaths. The title is a quote from a Roman writer, and translates as: it is sweet and right to die for your country. The poem describes a group of soldiers stumbling to reach a rest area:

War poet, Wilfred Owen

> Bent double, like old beggars under sacks,
> Knock-kneed, coughing like hags, we cursed through
>   sludge,
> Till on the haunting flares we turned our backs
> And towards our distant rest began to trudge.

When the men are suddenly gassed, Owen shows the reader a man dying from the gas. His pain and suffering are far from glorious:

> If you could hear, at every jolt, the blood
> Come gargling from the froth-corrupted lungs,
> Obscene as cancer, bitter as the cud
> Of vile, incurable sores on innocent tongues, –
> My friend, you would not tell with such high zest
> To children ardent for some desperate glory,
> The old Lie: Dulce et decorum est
> Pro patria mori.

Wilfred Owen was killed on November 4, 1918, just one week before the war ended. Church bells were ringing to celebrate Armistice Day when his parents received a telegram announcing his death. His poems are a chilling reminder of the suffering and pity of war.

A CHANGED WORLD

As soldiers returned home, many people were anxious to put the heartache and hardship of the war behind them, and get on with their lives. The cost of the war meant that governments faced massive debts, and everyone had to adjust to a future without the millions of men who had died. Life in the 1920s was going to be tough, but people wanted a reason to be cheerful again.

These children are using bundles of worthless German money as building blocks. Other people used the banknotes as fire lighters for their stoves.

Back to work?

During the war, agriculture and industry had expanded to meet the needs of the armed forces. This meant that many workers, including thousands of women, earned better wages and enjoyed greater social freedom than ever before. Soldiers returning home from the front were promised they could come back to work. But, as wartime industries were dismantled, there weren't so many jobs to go around. Women were expected to give up their jobs and go back home. For those left to support their families on a small war widow's pension, this was especially difficult. Government help for ex-servicemen left unemployed or disabled was little better. Many were forced onto the streets, and had to scrape a living by busking or selling trinkets. It was hardly the heroes' welcome they had expected to come home to.

INTERNET LINK

For a link to a website where you can read about the highs and lows of life during the Roaring Twenties, go to **www.usborne-quicklinks.com**

Worthless money

With many Germans already at starvation point as a result of the wartime blockades, the post-war reparations kept much of the population in poverty. The German government had no goods to trade with, so they simply printed more money to pay the Allies. This was a complete disaster. The more money they printed, the less it was worth. This is known as hyperinflation. By 1923, it was so bad that people suddenly found their life savings weren't even worth enough to buy a loaf of bread.

These people in Berlin are so poor, they are waiting in a bread line for free bread from the government, 1923.

Making good

Gradually, life became more prosperous, especially in America. Lessons learned from wartime industry – such as more efficient methods of mass-production – helped businesses to grow. Consumer goods such as radios, refrigerators and cars became cheaper and more widely available. Even in countries still struggling to recover from the war, young people wanted to have fun. Jazz music, dance halls, cinemas and revealing new women's clothes were all the rage, and the Hollywood movie industry boomed. This period became known as the Roaring Twenties.

International rescue

The people of Europe soon gained from America's growing prosperity. In 1923, the US government arranged massive loans for Germany to help businesses and fund war reparations to the Allies. Money flowed in to Europe, boosting industry and creating jobs. This took people out of unemployment and helped them to repair war damage. People began to feel things were getting better.

As their lives improved, many people had more leisure time than ever before. This British car advertisement from 1930 shows a family on an outing in the countryside.

Boom and bust

In 1929, the US stock market, based on Wall Street in New York, crashed. Millions of people lost their investments; banks closed down; companies folded and people lost their jobs. Families all across America abandoned their homes and went in search of work. As the American government called in their loans, the world fell into a financial depression, which would cause years of high unemployment and hardship.

SOLDIERS' STORIES

Like the war poets, many novelists, playwrights and journalists came home from the war feeling it was their duty to write about their experiences. Some were so disturbed by the fighting, that it changed the way they looked at the world. They had to find new ways of writing to describe the terrible things they had seen.

In the field

One of the few novels published by a soldier during the war was *Le Feu* (*Under Fire*) by the French writer Henri Barbusse. Describing the war as a senseless and horrific ordeal, it caused outrage in France when it appeared in bookstores, in 1916. Barbusse had been a patriot, and volunteered to fight. But he was so shocked by the confusion and misery he saw on the battlefield he became a pacifist.

This letter, from a chaplain serving on the Western Front, gives a vivid picture of the difficulties of trench warfare.

Letters home

During the war, newspapers had been so heavily censored and laden with propaganda, that many people didn't trust them. Letters from the front were censored too – sensitive details were cut or blacked out – but they gave readers a better sense of the mood in the trenches. After the war, some soldiers and nurses published their wartime letters and diaries for a public hungry to find out what it had really been like at the front.

INTERNET LINK

For a link to a website where you can find out more about literature and journalism from the First World War, or to see the trailer for the 1930 movie version of *All Quiet on the Western Front*, go to **www.usborne-quicklinks.com**

Warrior writers

Different writers who had taken part in the fighting had very different responses to the war. Two British books – Edmund Blunden's *Undertones of War* and Robert Graves's *Goodbye to All That* – presented the conflict as a hellish but necessary duty. But the German writer Ernst Jünger took a very a different tone. In his book *In Stahlgewittern* (*In Storms of Steel*) he praised the soldier's noble way of life and the excitement of battle. Another German, Erich Maria Remarque, produced a powerful anti-war book, *Im Westen Nichts Neues* (*All Quiet on the Western Front*). It followed a group of young volunteers through their nightmare in the trenches and their difficulties adjusting to life after the war.

A scene from the 1930 movie version of *All Quiet on the Western Front*

New directions

Some writers believed a whole generation had been cheated into fighting in the war and were then destroyed by it. One of them was the American Ernest Hemingway. He had been wounded in Italy, driving an ambulance behind the trenches. While living in Paris in the 1920s, he wrote about his wartime experiences in his book, *A Farewell to Arms*. In it, he explained that – for him – "words, such as glory, honor, courage" had lost their old meaning. To describe the world after the war, he had to come up with a new style of writing, using stark and brutal prose, which struck a chord with many war-weary readers.

Haunting memories

Many writers who had served during the war were haunted by the memories of the fighting. The sights and sounds of battle could suddenly resurface in their books – even those set in other worlds and times. J.R.R. Tolkien fought at Verdun and the Somme. In *The Lord of the Rings*, he described a swampy wasteland called the Dead Marshes. The bodies of slain warriors lay hidden in its murky waters, like the dead soldiers of a First World War no-man's-land, lost in their thousands in the mud.

The Harvest of Battle, by Christopher Nevinson. The flooded, muddy battlefield in this painting resembles Tolkein's description of the Dead Marshes in *The Lord of the Rings*.

VISIONS OF WAR

Many artists had served as soldiers during the war. Some governments even employed official war artists, photographers and film-makers to keep a visual record of the action. But some of the most powerful images of the war were produced after the fighting had ended.

The lonely dead

Taking pictures in the trenches was difficult and dangerous, and there were strict limits on where photographers were allowed to take their cameras. So there are very few pictures that show the intensity of battle. Many images of dead soldiers were censored or destroyed – in respect for their families and to keep morale strong at home. Those that were printed in newspapers usually showed lonely corpses in no-man's-land or one or two bodies sprawled in a trench. Looking at these pictures, it's hard to believe that thousands of men died every day of the war.

Charlie Chaplin as a soldier in the trenches, in his 1918 movie, *Shoulder Arms*. He carries an unusual kit, which includes a mouse trap, a cheese-grater and a tin bath.

INTERNET LINK

For links to websites where you can find out more about art, photography and movies of the First World War, go to **www.usborne-quicklinks.com**

John Singer Sargent's painting *Gassed*, shows British troops injured and blinded after a gas attack.

Photo stories

Some photographers were determined to show the terror and thrill of battle, even if they had to bend the truth to do it. The Australian, Frank Hurley, blended images of explosions, men and planes into a single photo. Critics attacked these 'collages' and called Hurley a fake, but his pictures are still among the most powerful of the war.

Crisis and comedy

Cinematography was a new art at the start of the 20th century, but this didn't stop the British filming their 'big push' at the Somme. Combining real footage of infantry leaving the trenches with staged action scenes, *The Battle of the Somme* was a massive hit when it was released in August 1916. But it showed few of the true horrors of the war.

Charlie Chaplin's *Shoulder Arms* took a more comic approach to the fighting. Playing an awkward American soldier, Chaplin disguised himself as a tree to spy behind enemy lines and ended the conflict by kidnapping the Kaiser.

A detail from *Skat Players* by Otto Dix. This shocking painting and collage depicts three crippled and mutilated ex-soldiers, playing cards.

War hungry

Otto Dix was a German painter who had volunteered to fight in the trenches, hungry for adventure. He won medals for his bravery, but the war sickened and haunted him. As Germany pieced itself together after the Armistice, Dix began painting the maimed ex-servicemen he saw begging on the streets. To many people they were an unwelcome reminder of the past, but Dix was determined that people should not be allowed to ignore their continued suffering.

AN UNHAPPY PEACE

Everyone had hoped that the Great War would be the war to end all wars. But, tragically, the post-war peace treaties created more problems than they solved. By 1919, people had even begun to refer to the recent conflict as the *First World War*, as a second one began to seem likely. The 1920s and 1930s were troubled decades. International resentments simmered, strikes and protests flared up, and governments around the world came under attack.

The Russian government used propaganda posters like this one to persuade people to work hard for their national industries.

This young Bolshevik volunteer is armed with a carbine gun and has two grenades in his gunbelt.

Winds of change

The experience of the First World War had made people in many countries think again about what kind of government they wanted to lead them. The chaos and hardship of the post-war years only added to these doubts. All around the world, people were throwing out reigning royal families, emperors and elected governments, and putting new leaders in their place. In some countries, this process was slow and peaceful; but in others, violence and force held sway. Either way, these changes created countless international suspicions, tensions and conflicts.

The red menace

While western Europe was slowly recovering, in Russia, rival groups fought savagely for power. Lenin's Bolsheviks finally gained control in 1921, and renamed their country the Soviet Union. By this time it was in chaos. Poor food distribution meant that as many as seven million people had died of starvation. To rebuild the country, politicians set high targets for industry and agriculture, and severe punishments for workers who didn't meet them. Anyone who dared to criticize the government was disposed of – killed or banished to the remote and desolate region of Siberia. But this harsh repression went on in secret. To the rest of the world, the Soviet Union seemed to be working.

Outposts of empire

In many of the European colonies which had sent troops to fight in the war, people began to question what their European rulers had done to deserve their support. In India, Africa and Australia, people started to push for the right to rule themselves. The USA provided inspiration for them: it had once been a British colony, but was now independent and was fast becoming the most powerful nation in the world. As America grew in strength and wealth, the huge empires of France and Britain began to decline.

Indian demands for independence were led by Mohandas 'Mahatma' Gandhi, who believed in non-violent protest. In this photograph, he addresses crowds of devoted followers during talks with British officials in India, 1931.

An age of extremes

The years after the war saw the rise of extreme political groups, who blamed their countries' problems on inefficient democratic governments. They wanted to put military dictators in charge, and were prepared to use violence to get their way. One of the first dictators to sweep to power was the leader of the Italian Fascist party, Benito Mussolini, in 1922. In Germany, Adolf Hitler – the leader of an extreme racist party, known as the Nazis – gained control in 1933. Mussolini and Hitler promised an end to unemployment and poverty. They planned to build up their nations' armies and conquer new empires. Both these dictators, and Lenin's successor, Josef Stalin, kept tight controls over people's lives by regulating the media and brutally suppressing all opposition.

INTERNET LINK

For a link to a website where you can explore the lives of Gandhi, Mussolini, Hitler or Stalin, go to **www.usborne-quicklinks.com**

Nazis parade through Nuremberg, in Germany, in 1930. The man at the front is carrying the party flag, known as the Swastika.

The 20-year cease-fire

In the Balkans and eastern Europe, disputes arose constantly. The League of Nations tried to keep the peace, usually unsuccessfully as it didn't have an army to enforce its rulings. Against this background, it wasn't surprising that both politicians and civilians lost faith in a lasting peace. People began to talk of the post-war treaties as nothing more than a 20-year cease-fire. Tragically, they were proved right. In 1939, only 20 years after the Paris Peace Conference that had ended the war, another devastating global conflict began: the Second World War.

LEST WE FORGET

As many as 21 million men, women and children lost their lives in the First World War. No previous conflict in history had caused so many casualties. Throughout the war, people worked to make sure the dead were treated with respect – even when the fighting made this difficult. But, when peace came, nations across the world made more lasting memorials to those who had died.

A German painting of a soldier's grave, in a poppy field in Flanders, 1919

Killed in action

The sheer numbers killed meant that it just wasn't possible for most countries to transport their dead back, to be buried at home. Many of the men who died in battle had to be buried hastily at night, just behind the front line. Where possible, these graves were given simple markers, and armies tried to keep a record of who was buried where, but many bodies were simply never found.

Set in stone

In Britain, France and Germany, almost every family lost at least one member. Grieving relatives needed to feel that their loved ones had not been forgotten. So, after the war, land close to the battlefields was set aside for cemeteries.

Many survivors felt that no one grave should look more important than any another, regardless of the rank, race or religion of the dead person. So each was marked by a simple headstone that recorded a name and a date. Back at home, many cities and local communities around the world set up their own war memorials in the years after the war, carved with lists of names of all those who had died.

A crowd looks on as a British general stands in front of a war memorial he has just unveiled in central London, October 1925.

We will remember them

In the years following the war, November 11, the anniversary of the Armistice, was set aside as a day of remembrance. Many people were struck by the beautiful red poppies that began to cover the battlefields of Flanders, once the fighting had stopped. The poppy quickly became a powerful symbol of the First World War dead.

Now, on November 11 every year, people wear poppies and lay wreaths at war memorials all around the world, to remember those who have died in all wars, not just the First World War.

WHO'S WHO

Many people played a vital role in the events of the First World War. Here are some of the leading personalities from both sides. Names shown in *italic* type have an entry of their own, and words in *italics* are explained in the glossary on the following pages.

Allenby, Field Marshal Sir Edmund (1861-1936) commanded the British *cavalry* on the *Western Front* until 1917. After that, he was the Allied commander-in-chief in the Middle East, where he led the final campaign against the Turks in Palestine.

Brusilov, General Alexei (1853-1926) was a general in the Russian army. In 1916, he led a successful offensive against Austria-Hungary, and in 1917, *Alexander Kerensky* made him Russia's commander-in-chief.

Churchill, Winston (1874-1965) was Britain's first lord of the admiralty in 1914-15, and minister of *munitions* in 1917-18. He believed the navy could help to win the war on land, and was partly responsible for the disastrous Allied campaign in Gallipoli. In 1940, he became British prime minister.

Clemenceau, Georges (1841-1929) was the premier of France, 1917-1920. Nicknamed 'the Tiger' because of his aggressive negotiating skills. At Versailles, he was the most vocal in demanding strict punishment of the Germans.

Enver Pasha (1881-1922) was a former officer in the Turkish army, who underwent part of his training in Germany. He became leader of the Young Turks in 1908, and was their minister of war from 1914. After the war, Enver Pasha fled first to Germany, then to Russia, where he lived until his death.

Falkenhayn, General Erich von (1861-1922) was the German army's chief of general staff until 1916. *Kaiser Wilhelm II* held him responsible for huge numbers of German casualties at Ypres and Verdun, and replaced him with *Hindenberg* and Ludendorff in August 1916. He was transferred to the Balkans, where he swiftly defeated Rumania.

Feisal, Emir of Mecca (1885-1933) led the Arabs against the Turks and continued to argue for Arab independence after the war. In 1920, he claimed the throne in Syria, but was thrown out by the French who held the *mandate* there. A year later, after an offer from the British, he became the first king of Iraq.

Foch, Marshal Ferdinand (1851-1929) led the French forces at the Battle of the Somme. In 1918, he took overall command, of the combined Allied forces on the *Western Front*, where he helped to bring the Allies to victory.

Franz Ferdinand, Archduke (1863-1914) was the heir to the Austro-Hungarian throne. His assassination by Gavrilo Princip led to the outbreak of the war.

Franz Josef I, Emperor (1830-1916) ruled Austria-Hungary. When his nephew and heir, *Archduke Franz Ferdinand*, was assassinated, the Emperor declared war on Serbia for revenge. When he died in November 1916, his great-nephew, Karl I (1887-1922) took the throne, but was forced to step down two years later when the empire was broken up.

French, Field Marshal Sir John (later Earl French of Ypres) (1852-1925) was a former cavalryman and commander-in-chief of Britain's overseas army – the British Expeditionary Force – at the outbreak of the war. He lost his job in December 1915, after one of his own generals, *Haig*, whispered to King George V that the army had lost confidence in him.

Haig, Field Marshal Sir Douglas (later Earl Haig of Bemersyde) (1861-1928) took command of the British army on the *Western Front* from *French*. His tactics have been attacked for their cost in human life, particularly at the Battle of the Somme.

Hindenberg, Field Marshal Paul von (1847-1934) was called out of retirement, aged 67, when the war broke out. With his right-hand man, General Erich Ludendorff, he masterminded Germany's final Spring Offensive on the *Western Front* in 1918. He was president of Germany from 1925 until his death, and appointed Adolf Hitler as his chancellor in 1933.

Jellicoe, Admiral of the Fleet Earl John (1859-1935) was commander-in-chief of the British Grand Fleet. At the Battle of Jutland, his tactics were criticized for being too cautious.

Joffre, Marshal Joseph (1852-1931) was commander-in-chief of the French army in 1914, credited with having saved Paris.

Kemal, Mustafa (1881-1938) was a Turkish army commander, whose leadership at Gallipoli made him a national hero. After the war, he led the Turkish resistance to Allied occupation and set up a provisional government. In 1924, he abolished the Ottoman sultanate and became the first president of the Turkish Republic. In 1934, he was given the title *Atatürk* – meaning 'Father of the Turks' – by the Turkish National Assembly.

Kerensky, Alexander (1881-1970) became Russia's minister of war after the fall of *Tsar Nicholas II*, then head of the Russian government. His unpopular decision to continue fighting the war, led to a second *revolution* in Russia. In November 1917, he and his government were overthrown by the Bolsheviks, and he spent the rest of his life in exile.

Kitchener, Field Marshal Lord, Earl Kitchener of Kartoum (1850-1916) was British secretary of state for war, and built up the British army. He died in 1916, on a ship that struck a mine.

Lawrence, Thomas Edward (1888-1935) was a British *intelligence* officer, known as Lawrence of Arabia because of his fervent support for Arab independence. After the war, he published *Seven Pillars of Wisdom*, his account of the Arab Revolt. He died in 1935, after a motorcycle accident, but became a legend when his story was made into a Hollywood movie, *Lawrence of Arabia*, in 1962.

Lenin (1870-1924) was born Vladimir Ilyich Ulyanov, but changed his name during his student days. In 1905, he played a leading role in a revolt against the Tsar. After that, Lenin lived in exile in Switzerland. In 1917, he returned to Russia to lead the Bolshevik *Revolution*, becoming the new head of government. He died of brain disease in 1924. His body was preserved and has been on public display in Moscow ever since.

Lettow-Vorbeck, Colonel (later Major General) Paul von (1870-1964) led the German army's campaign in East Africa. He used *guerrilla* tactics to fight an Allied force far bigger than his own, and was the only commander to last the entire war without ever being defeated. After the war, he served in the German parliament, where he opposed the Nazis.

Lloyd George, David (1863-1945) was the leading member of the British government throughout the war. He became prime minister in 1916, and led the post-war peace talks in Paris, along with *Clemenceau* and *Wilson*.

Moltke, General Helmuth von (1848-1916) was responsible for putting the German army's Schlieffen Plan into action in August 1914. When it failed, he was replaced by *Falkenhayn*.

Nicholas II, Tsar (1868-1918) came to the Russian throne in 1894. During the war, he took command of the Russian army, while his wife, the Tsarina, managed affairs at home. Both were unsuccessful and became increasingly unpopular, until the Tsar was overthrown in March 1917. The following year, the Tsar and his family were executed by Bolshevik soldiers.

Nivelle, General Robert (1856-1924) was an artilleryman in the French army who replaced *Joffre* in command of the French on the *Western Front* in 1916-1917. But, when his ambitious offensive in the spring of 1917 failed, many of his troops *mutinied* and he was replaced by *Pétain*.

Pershing, General John Joseph 'Black Jack' (1860-1948) led the American army in Europe. After the war, he was given the title General of the Armies, a rank previously only held by President George Washington.

Pétain, General Henri Philippe (1856-1951) was credited with saving Verdun in 1916, and became a French national hero as a result. In May 1917, he became French commander-in-chief, until being replaced by *Foch* in 1918. During the Second World War, he led the French government in Vichy, under German *occupation*. He was later found guilty of treason for collaborating with the Nazis and died in prison.

Richthofen, Captain Baron Manfred von (1892-1918) was a German fighter pilot, known as the Red Baron, and the most successful air 'ace' of the war, with 80 confirmed kills. He was shot down over the *Western Front*, in April 1918, aged 25.

Scheer, Admiral Reinhard (1863-1928) masterminded the German naval attacks against Britain in the North Sea, and commanded the High Seas Fleet at the Battle of Jutland.

Smuts, General Jan (1870-1950) was a South African who fought in the Boer War against the British, but who led the Allied forces in Africa during the First World War. He became prime minister of South Africa in 1919.

Spee, Admiral Count Maximilian von (1861-1914) commanded the German fleet in the Pacific. He waged a form of naval *guerrilla warfare*, targeting the Allies' merchant ships and trading ports. His fleet was eventually defeated at the Battle of the Falklands, when Spee went down with his ship.

Wilson, Thomas Woodrow (1856-1924) President of the United States, 1913-1920. He kept his country out of the war until 1917, when German *U-boats* began sinking US ships. In January 1918, he produced a 14-point plan for peace, which provided the basis for the *Armistice* later that year. Mainly responsible for establishing the League of Nations, he was bitterly disappointed when the US Senate refused to join.

Wilhelm II, Kaiser (1859-1941) Emperor of Germany, 1888-1918. The Kaiser spent the early years of his reign building up the strength of his armed forces, especially the navy. Officially, Wilhelm was the head of the German military throughout the war. But, in reality, he lacked the necessary skill and experience, so was little more than a figurehead. At the end of the war, he was forced to *abdicate* and spent the rest of his life in exile in the Netherlands.

INTERNET LINK

For a link to a website where you can find out about some of the other leading personalities of the war, including royalty, politicians, military commanders, writers and artists, go to **www.usborne-quicklinks.com**

GLOSSARY

This glossary explains some of the words you may come across when reading about the First World War. If a word used in an entry has a separate entry of its own, it is shown in *italic* type.

abdication Giving up a position of power, usually that of king, queen or emperor.

airship A large air balloon which can be steered and is propelled by engines.

Allied Powers The countries that fought against the *Central Powers* in the First World War. The main Allied nations were Britain, France, Russia, Italy and the United States of America.

armistice An agreement between warring nations or parties to stop fighting.

arms race The competition between nations to produce and stockpile bigger, better and more weapons than each other.

artillery Large but transportable guns used in land fighting.

auxiliary A person who works to support the armed forces, but who isn't directly engaged in combat.

barrage Steady *artillery* fire against an enemy force.

battalion A unit in the armed forces, comprising a large number of soldiers who are organized into several different groups and the leaders who control these groups. Usually numbering about 850 men.

battleship A large, heavily-armed and fortified warship.

bayonet A long, sharp blade designed to be attached to the end of a rifle for use in hand-to-hand fighting.

blockade An attempt by one warring party to obstruct the passage of troops, food and other supplies into land owned or controlled by their opponents.

cavalry Soldiers who fight on horseback.

cease-fire A period of truce, when opposing forces agree to stop firing at one another. A cease-fire is either temporary, or the first step in the process of making permanent peace.

censorship The control or suppression, often by a government, of information that may threaten its goals.

Central Powers The nations that fought against the *Allied Powers* in the First World War. The Central Powers were Germany, Austria-Hungary, the Turkish empire and Bulgaria.

civilian Anyone who is not a member of the armed forces.

colony A geographical area under the political control of another country.

conscription Compulsory recruitment of citizens into the armed forces.

cooperative A system in which workers and consumers share ownership and profits of a business.

cruiser A large warship that is faster than a *battleship*, but with less firepower, and not as heavily fortified.

democracy A political system in which citizens can freely elect people to represent them in government.

depression A period of steep price rises, when many businesses fail, leading to mass unemployment and poverty.

dictatorship Government of a country or empire by a ruler who holds unlimited power.

dreadnought A type of *battleship* mounted with guns and powered by turbines, named after the first of its kind, HMS *Dreadnought*.

Eastern Front The *front lines* in central and eastern Europe which lay to the east of Germany and Austria-Hungary.

empire A group of countries or territories under the control of another country.

espionage The use of spies to obtain information, particularly political or military secrets.

front line The boundary along which opposing armies face each other.

genocide The systematic extermination of a group of people based on distinctions of race, nationality, ethnicity or religion.

grenade A small explosive weapon thrown by a soldier.

guerrilla warfare The method of fighting by launching surprise attacks which are relatively small and scattered, usually used against a larger or more professional army.

home front Anyone or anything in the home country during a foreign war. In times of *Total War*, the contribution and efforts of those on the home front is seen to play a vital role in the war's outcome.

howitzer A type of *artillery* cannon capable of firing *shells* high into the air to increase their range and impact.

hyperinflation An ongoing extreme rise in prices, causing the currency effectively to lose its value. Hyperinflation often leads to a period of financial *depression*.

infantry Soldiers who fight mostly on foot.

intelligence Secret military information about an enemy, often gathered by *espionage*.

jihad An Islamic holy war waged against non-Muslims.

machine gun A gun that can fire bullets very quickly without needing to be reloaded.

mandate A territory controlled and administered by a member state of the League of Nations after the war.

marine A type of soldier who fights on land and at sea.

merchant ship A non-military ship which transports goods to be bought and sold.

mobilization Action taken in preparation for going to war; 'mobilizing the troops' means organizing soldiers and getting them into position ready for combat.

morale The collective spirit or confidence of a group of people, especially in the armed forces.

munitions Military equipment including *artillery* and ammunition such as bullets, bombs and *shells*.

mutiny A revolt against the person or persons in charge by those who are supposed to obey them.

nationalism The belief among people who live in the same region, and who have the same culture, language or religion, that they would benefit from forming their own nation.

no-man's-land The stretch of open, unoccupied land separating the *front lines* of two warring sides.

occupation Seizing and taking control of an area.

officer Usually a senior member of the armed forces.

over the top In *trench warfare*, the act of climbing over the *parapet* of a *trench* into *no-man's-land* in order to charge at the enemy.

parapet The top edge of a *trench* wall facing the enemy, usually lined with sandbags.

patriotism Loving one's country and being prepared to fight for it.

periscope A vertical tube with prisms at each end that allows you to see something from a position a long way below, used in submarines and sometimes in trenches.

private The lowest rank of soldier in the armed forces.

propaganda Information that is systematically spread to promote or damage a political cause.

rationing Strict control of how much food and other goods someone is allowed.

reconnaissance An exploration and inspection of an area to gather information.

reparations Payments made by Germany to several Allied nations after its defeat in the First World War, justified as being compensation for causing the war.

revolution The overthrow of a leader or government by the people, usually as a result of violent struggle.

salient A piece of land held by one warring party that bulges into its enemy's territory.

sentry A person charged with the job of keeping guard and watching for danger.

shell A hollow missile containing explosives.

shell shock Mental illness or breakdown caused by participation in active warfare. Doctors now recognize this as a form of post-traumatic stress disorder.

shrapnel Small pieces of metal scattered by the explosion of a bomb, *shell* or mine.

sniper A rifleman who takes shots at enemy soldiers from a concealed position.

stalemate A situation where neither side can win, and no further action can be taken.

submarine A ship that can travel under the water for long periods, widely used for the first time in the First World War.

'Tommy' A nickname used to refer to British soldiers, from 'Thomas Atkins' – commonly used as a sample name when demonstrating how to fill in military forms.

torpedo A self-propelled, explosive device which travels through water and can be launched from a plane or a ship.

Total War A type of warfare which involves entire nations, including *civilians* on the *home front*, rather than just those directly engaged in the fighting.

trench A deep, fortified ditch.

trench warfare A type of warfare in which opposing armies dig *trenches* facing one another along most of the *front line*. Trenches are easy to defend but difficult to attack, so trench warfare often ends in *stalemate*.

U-boat A German *submarine*. The name comes from *unterseeboot*, which means 'undersea boat' in German.

Western Front The *front lines* which lay to the west of Germany, in Belgium and Northern France.

Zeppelin A tube-shaped *airship* invented by the German, Count Ferdinand von Zeppelin, and used for *reconnaissance* and bombing during the war.

INDEX

ACKNOWLEDGEMENTS

Every effort has been made to trace and acknowledge ownership of copyright. If any rights have been omitted, the publishers offer to rectify this in any future editions following notification. The publishers are grateful to the following individuals and organizations for their permission to reproduce material on the following pages: (IWM=Imperial War Museum, t=top, m=middle, b=bottom, l=left, r=right)

Front cover (t) © Hulton-Deutsch Collection/CORBIS, (m) © Hulton Archive/Getty Images, (b) © Bettmann/CORBIS,
Front and back covers © Digital Vision/Getty Images; **Back cover** (t) IWM Q1208, (b) © Hulton Archive/Getty Images;

p1 The Art Archive/IWM; **pp2–3** IWM Q194; **pp4–5** IWM Q93351; **pp6–7** © David Hughes/Robert Harding/Getty Images; **p8** Scherl/SV-Bilderdienst; **p10** (bl) © Christel Gerstenberg/CORBIS, (tr) IWM Q81824; **pp10–11** The Naval Historical Foundation, Washington, USA; **p12** (tr) IWM Q81831, (br) IWM Q91840; **p13** © Time Life Pictures/Getty Images; **p14** (tr) © Topical Press Agency/Hulton Archive/Getty Images; **pp14–15** © Bettmann/CORBIS; **p15** (br) © Gunn & Stuart/Hulton Archive/Getty Images; **p16** (tr) IWM Q65817, (b) IWM Q53248; **p17** (t) Robert Hunt Library, (br) Robert Hunt Library; **pp18–19** Jacques Moreau/Archives Larousse, Paris, France/Giraudon/The Bridgeman Art Library; **p20** (tr) IWM Q57380; **pp20–21** © Topical Press Agency/Hulton Archive/Getty Images; **p21** (tr) IWM Q57287; **p22** (tr) IWM ART1656; **pp22–23** Roger-Viollet/Topfoto; **pp24–25** IWM Q49104; **p26** (tr) IWM Q27870; **pp26–27** IWM CO747; **p27** (tr) © Hulton Archive/Getty Images; **p28** (tr) Mary Evans Picture Library, (br) © Hulton-Deutsch Collection/CORBIS; **pp28–29** IWM CO872; **p30** (tr) IWM Q19538; **pp30–31** © Spencer Arnold/Hulton Archive/Getty Images; **p32** (tr) IWM PST2734, (b) © Bettmann/CORBIS; **p33** (t) © Hulton Archive/Getty Images, (b) IWM; **p34** (tr) © akg-images/ullstein bild, (bl) ©2003 Topham Picturepoint/TopFoto.co.uk; **p35** © Hulton Archive/Getty Images; **pp36–37** Robert Hunt Library; **p38** (bl) IWM PST2756; **pp38–39** IWM Q20896; **pp40–41** IWM Q45776; **p41** (tr) IWM Q15681; **p42** (tr) IWM Q23732; **pp42–43** © Hulton-Deutsch Collection/CORBIS; **p43** (tr) © Hulton Archive/Getty Images; **p44** (b) © Cheryl Koralik/Photonica/Getty Images; **pp44–45** (t) Armin T. Wegner © Wallstein Verlag, Germany. All rights reserved. Used by Permission; **p45** (br) © 2006 Topham Picturepoint/ TopFoto.co.uk; **pp46–47** © MPI/Hulton Archive/Getty Images; **pp48–49** © Hulton-Deutsch Collection/CORBIS; **p50** (b) IWM Q51650; **p51** (tr) IWM Q11586, (br) IWM Q55085; **p52** (tr) The Art Archive/Private Collection Newbury, (b) IWM Q8382; **p53** © Hulton Archive/Getty Images; **p54** (tr) © Bettmann/CORBIS; **pp54–55** © CORBIS; **p55** (br) © Mary Evans Picture Library/Alamy; **p56** (tr) SHEILA TERRY/SCIENCE PHOTO LIBRARY; **pp56–57** IWM Q58481; **p57** (bl) IWM Q27226; **p58** (bl) IWM Q28440, (tr) IWM PST3521; **pp58–59** © Hulton-Deutsch Collection/CORBIS; **p60** (tr) Mary Evans Picture Library; **pp60–61** © CORBIS; **p62** (tr) © Bettmann/CORBIS; **pp62–63** IWM Q115126; **pp64–65** © Hulton-Deutsch Collection/CORBIS; **p66** (tr) © Hulton Archive/Getty Images; **pp66–67** Musee d'Histoire Contemporaine, B.D.I.C., Paris, France, Archives Charmet/The Bridgeman Art Library; **p68** (tr) © Hulton Archive/Getty Images; **pp68–69** IWM Q18121; **p70** (l) IWM Q27025A; **pp70–71** IWM Q23584; **p72** © David Wall/Alamy; **p73** (tr) IWM Q107381, (ml) © George Hall/CORBIS, (tr) © Hulton Archive/Getty Images, (bl) IWM Q754; **pp74–75** IWM Q70167; **p76** IWM Q24047; **p77** (tr) IWM Q70742, (br) IWM E(AUS)715; **p78** (b) © CORBIS, (tr) IWM PST2766; **p79** (t) IWM Q27255, (br) IWM Q106252; **p80** IWM Q54534; **pp80–81** (t) RIA Novosti Photo Library; **p82** © Underwood & Underwood/CORBIS; **p83** (bl) The National Archives, UK, (r) © Blue Lantern Studio/CORBIS; **p84** (tr) IWM Q46094; **pp84–85** IWM Q58863; **p85** (r) IWM Q24168; **pp86–87** IWM Q69408; **p88** (bl) © Bettmann/CORBIS, (tr) IWM ART5219/Reproduced with kind permission from the Nevinson estate/The Bridgeman Art Library; **p89** RIA Novosti Photo Library; **p90** (tr) © Bettmann/CORBIS; **pp90–91** © Bettmann/CORBIS; **p91** (bl) © Hulton-Deutsch Collection/CORBIS, (tr) TopFoto/HIP/ TopFoto.co.uk; **p92** © Three Lions/Hulton Archive/Getty Images; **p93** (l) © Bettmann/CORBIS, (tr) Courtesy of The Library of Congress, LC cph-3g03859, (br) © CORBIS; **p94** (tr) IWM Q5943; **pp94–95** IWM E(AUS)001220; **pp96–97** © Bettmann/CORBIS; **p98** (tr) US National Archives and Records Administration; **pp98–99** (b) The Art Archive / IWM; **p99** (tr) © Time Life Pictures/Getty Images; **p100** (bl) IWM Q12616, (tr) IWM Q13213B; **pp100–101** Australian War Memorial, Negative Number B00256; **p102** (bl) © Hulton-Deutsch Collection/CORBIS, (tr) IWM Q43225; **pp102–103** © Hulton-Deutsch Collection/CORBIS; **pp104–105** IWM Q9580; **pp106–107** © Bettmann/CORBIS; **p107** (tr) IWM HU55555; **p108** (tr) © Underwood & Underwood/CORBIS; **p109** (bl) © Bettmann/CORBIS; **p110** (tr) Library Kings College Cambridge/RCB/V/1 folio 17: 'The Soldier'; **pp110–111** IWM Q005242; **p111** (r) IWM Q79045; **p112** (tr) © Hulton-Deutsch Collection/CORBIS; **pp112–113** © Bettmann/CORBIS; **p113** (tr) Mary Evans Picture Library; **p114** (tr) © American Stock/Hulton Archive/Getty Images; **pp114–115** IWM ART1460; **p115** (tr) The Art Archive/Private Collection/Dagli Orti/© DACS 2006; **p116** (tr) IWM ART16695; **pp116–117** IWM ART1921; **p117** (ml) © John Springer Collection/CORBIS; **p118** (l) © P. Otsup/Slava Katamidze Collection/Hulton Archive/Getty Images, (tr) Anon; **p119** (t) © Bettmann/CORBIS, (b) © POPPERFOTO/Alamy; **p120** (tr) Mary Evans Picture Library; **pp120–121** IWM Q42446

Half-title page: Soldiers walk through the flooded Ancre Valley, in northern France, 1916.
Title page: Soldiers from the 2nd Auckland Battalion (New Zealand) pose in a trench near Flers, during the Battle of the Somme in September 1916.

Picture research: Ruth King

Cartography: Craig Asquith

Digital imaging: Keith Furnival

Editorial consultant: Paul Dowswell

Additional editorial contributions: Sarah Khan, Hazel Maskell and Abigail Wheatley

For more information about the Imperial War Museum, go to www.iwm.org.uk

INTERNET LINKS

Throughout this book, we have recommended interesting websites where you can find out more about the First World War and watch movie clips, play games and view interactive exhibits. For links to the sites, go to the Usborne Quicklinks Website, where you will find links to all the sites.

1. In your computer's web browser, type the address **www.usborne-quicklinks.com** to go to the Usborne Quicklinks Website.

2. At the Usborne Quicklinks Website, type the keywords: **world war one**

3. Type the page number of the link you want to visit. When the link appears, click on it to go to the recommended site.

Websites to visit

Here are some of the things you can do on the websites recommended in this book:

• View animated timelines and maps of the major battles of the war

• Listen to eyewitness accounts of life at the front

• Watch film footage of soldiers digging a trench on the Western Front

• Explore photo galleries of tanks, airships, battleships and fighter planes

• Try your hand at delivering an important message in the trenches

Site availability

The links in Usborne Quicklinks are regularly updated, but occasionally you may get a message that a site is unavailable. This might be temporary, so try again later, or even the next day.

Staying safe online

Make sure you follow these simple rules to keep you safe online:

Always ask an adult's permission before connecting to the Internet.

Never give out information about yourself, such as your real name, address, phone number or school.

If a site asks you to log in or register by typing your name or email address, ask permission from an adult first.

If you receive an email from someone you don't know, don't reply to it. Tell an adult.

Net help

For information and help using the Internet, go to the Net Help are on the Usborne Quicklinks Website. You'll find information about "plug-ins" – small free programs you may need to play sound, videos or animations. You probably already have these, but if not, you can download them for free from Quicklinks Net Help. You can also find information about computer viruses and advice on anti-virus software to protect your computer.

Adults

The websites described in this book are regularly reviewed, but websites can change and Usborne Publishing is not responsible for the content on any site other than its own.

We recommend that children are supervised while on the Internet, that they do not use Internet chat rooms, and that filtering software is used to block unsuitable material. You can find more information on Internet safety at the Usborne Quicklinks Website.